Dwayne's Guitar Lessons
Presents:

Lead Guitar Shredder

A Comprehensive Training Guide

By
Guitar Teacher
Dwayne Jenkins

Introduction

Lead guitar shredding is an exhilarating and skillful art form that captivates audiences with its fast-paced, intricate solos. This technique, often associated with rock and heavy metal music, showcases a guitarist's technical prowess and creativity.

This style of lead guitar playing emphasises speed, precision, and dexterity. It involves rapid picking, complex guitar solos, and advanced techniques that push the boundaries of conventional guitar playing.

Shredding guitar is not just about playing fast; it is also about understanding theory and scales. Certain concepts allow you to convey emotion through high-speed, creative musical passages.

To become proficient as a lead guitar shredder, you need to master concepts associated with this complex style of music. Such techniques as alternate picking, tremolo picking, sweep picking, guitar licks, phrasing, and above all else, timing.

You also need to develop patience, persistence, and be dedicated to hours of practice. This type of art form requires discipline, concentration, and focus above the norm. This is because of the speed at which you are playing.

This comrehensive training course will guide you through the techniques, concepts, and tools needed to excel proficiently at this art form. Speed and precision are the essence of lead guitar shredding.

It will also be recommended that you work with a metronome to develop timing and increase speed at an even tempo. Focus on developing solid practice habits to ensure clean playing and that each note is clear and distinct.

You will also need to dedicate time to listening to players who incorporate speed in their guitar solos. The repetition of the concepts presented will etch them in your mind, body, and soul, which will be needed for efficient playing.

So, if you're ready, grab your guitar and follow this guide like a map to a hidden treasure. Before you know it, you will be shredding guitar like you never thought possible. Good luck, and don't forget to have fun.

Sincerely, Dwayne Jenkins

Table of Contents

Chapter I: Lead Guitar Intro

Lesson 1: The lead guitarist

The role of the lead guitarist is to provide musical elements that complement the rhythm being provided by the bass player or the rhythm guitarist. His job is to expand the musical composition with riffs, melodies, and guitar solos.

The lead guitarist holds a pivotal part in the musical landscape. His role is not just about crafting solos and melodies, but also providing the listener with inspiration as he drives the narrative emotion of the song.

The ability to create lead lines that are compelling and memorable is the job of the lead guitarist. To elevate the sound, set the mood, and enhance the overall impact of the character of the song.

This not only requires technical skill, but also a deep understanding of the music being played, and the proper emotion can be expressed to complement the composition.

Within an ensemble setting, the lead guitarist collaborates closely with the other musicians to shape the overall sound. This is done through listening and complementing the rhythm section to create a cohesive musical experience.

Lesson 2: Types of lead guitars

When it comes to lead guitar playing, certain types of guitars are designed for this purpose. Any solid body electric guitar could do, but if you get one that's designed specifically for shredding purposes, you'll do better.

Shred-style guitars:

These types of guitars are specifically designed for this style of lead guitar playing. Lead guitar shred. Unlike traditional guitars like the Gibson Les Paul and the Fender Stratocaster, these have different features that cater to this type of playing.

#1# Guitar neck
These have a thinner profile for faster playing. As well as eliminating tension on the hand when doing so.

#2: Locking nut or tuners
These allow the guitar to stay in tune better when using the whammy bar that is attached to the bridge.

#3: Fretboard and frets
The fretboard is designed for faster playing, as well as the jumbo frets that help with expressing notes better.

#4: Pickups
These come equipped with humbucker pickups for a more robust guitar tone. Which allows your guitar solos to soar.

#6: Floating bridge
This type of bridge allows you to raise and lower the pitch to create jaw-dropping guitar sounds.

Make sure your guitar has all these features and you'll be set to shred!

Lesson 3: Types of amplifiers

Now that you have the correct type of guitar for lead guitar shredding, you need to get the correct type of amplifier. These come in many styles, and too many to list, but here are a couple of options.

Shred-style amplifiers:

#1: combo amplifiers

These incorporate both the amplifier head and speaker cabinet in one single unit. There are various types: solid-state, tube, and modeling amps. These are very popular because they are easily portable and work great in smaller spaces.

Here are two examples of combo amps. A Fender and a Marshall. These come in tube, modeling, and solid-state versions.

The other type of amplifier that works well is a stacked amplifier. This is where the amplifier and the speaker cabinet are not in one unit. They are separate. This allows for more options when creating your sound, because you can exchange them.

#2: Amp & cabinet separate

As you can see from these two pictures, the amps are similar but different. In the first picture, the amp and cabinet are the same, but in the second picture, the amp and speaker cabinet are different.

This is the benefit of separating the amplifier from the speaker cabinet. You can change them out to give you a different type of look and sound.

Make sure you have one of these types of amplifiers.

6

Lesson 4: Reading guitar tabs

When it comes to learning to play the guitar, there are two ways you can do it. You can do it, playing by ear, or you can do it by learning to read sheet music. Most people play by ear because sheet music can be confusing.

Enter guitar tabs. A basic form of sheet music that makes reading music notation easy. The reason for this is that it takes out the confusion by simplifying what you're reading.

Guitar tabs consist of 6 horizontal lines that represent the guitar strings. These will be from high to low. Meaning that your biggest string will be on the bottom line, and your smallest string will be on the top line.

The only thing to remember is that the lines are reversed from your guitar. The reason for this is that in sheet music, the lowest note will always be at the bottom. So you'll need to pay attention to this when reading it.

If you give it time and patience, you will soon see how reading guitar tabs can enhance and benefit your guitar playing.

Once you have the guitar lines concept down, you want to think in numbers. Why? Because numbers placed on the lines will represent which frets you're going to place your fingers on.

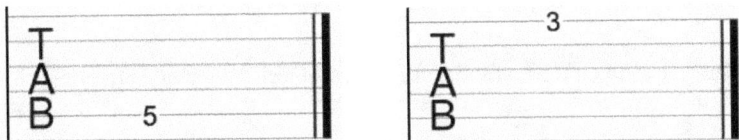

In these two examples above, we have a single note on a single string. The first one is the 5th fret on the 5th string, and the second one is the 3rd fret on the 1st string.

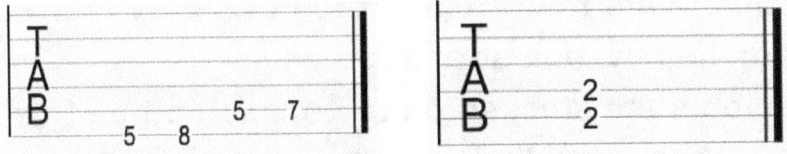

In these next two examples, we have two different notations. The first one is 4 individual notes on the 6th and 5th strings played one after another. The second one indicates 2 frets played together to form a chord. An E minor chord.

When the numbers are side by side, like in the first example, they are played one after another. But when they are stacked on top of each other, they are played together.

This is how single-note melodies and chords are indicated in guitar tabs. As we get further along with the training, I will show you more about how to read tabs and what the symbols in the tabs represent.

For now, I recommend you just try to remember a few things about the basics.

1. **The 6 lines represent the guitar strings.**
2. **The lines are upside down from your guitar.**
3. **The frets that you will place your fingers on will be indicated by numbers.**
4. **When numbers are read from left to right, they are played individually, one after another.**
5. **When numbers are stacked on top of each other, this indicates a chord, and they are played together.**

These are the fundamental principles of reading guitar tabs. If you can understand these basic concepts, everything in the following chapters will make more sense and be easier to play.

But it all comes down to you, and the time you put in to understanding these concepts. You also want to remember that music is a language, and just like reading any other type of language, there will be a learning curve.

Just be patient with yourself, and you'll get there. I promise.

Lesson 5: Learning finger exercises

Now, before we get to shredding on the guitar, we want to get our hands and fingers in shape. The best way to do this is through finger exercises that are practiced daily.

Not only will these help with getting and keeping your hands in shape for lead guitar shredding, but they will also help with forming and holding chords when playing rhythm guitar.

Finger exercise #1:

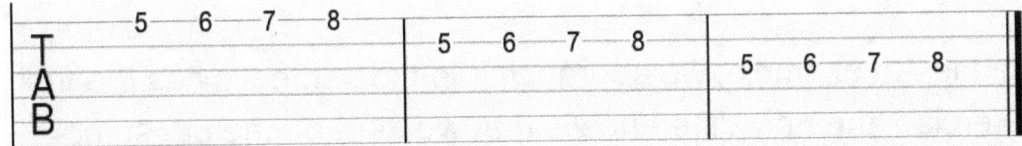

In this 1st example, you start at the 5th fret on the 1st string and span over the next 4 frets. Start with your index finger, and use all four as you move across all 6 strings.

Finger exercise #2:

In this 2nd example, we start on the 6th string and play it open. This is where you play the string without putting a finger on a fret. Follow the same example as the 1st exercise.

Finger exercise #3:

In this 3rd example, you start at the 2nd fret of the 1st string and proceed across strings instead of alongside them. This will help develop finger strength and independence.

Finger exercise #4:

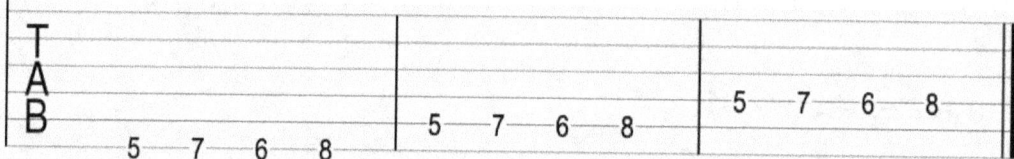

In this 4th example, we approach it in the same way as the first exercise; the only difference is that we start on the 6th string and change up the fingering.

Finger exercise #5:

In this last example, we move across the fretboard like before, but move up the fretboard in the process. This not only helps with finger independence but also with fretboard mastery.

Practice these, and get your fingers in shape for shredding!

Chapter I Summary

First, we learned about the role of the lead guitarist. This is very important to know, as there are certain things that the lead guitarist is responsible for in the musical landscape.

Second, we look at types of guitars that are best used for lead guitar shredding. This is important because the techniques used to play shred guitar will help you to have one that can easily assist you in executing them.

Third, we learn about the types of amplifiers that are best used for this style of playing. The guitar and amplifier are your two main tools of the trade, and the right ones can make all the difference when playing any style of music.

Fourth, we look at how to read guitar tabs. A simplified form of sheet music designed to allow you to spend more time playing and less time getting confused about the sheet music you're looking at. This is common with standard notation.

Lastly, we look at finger exercises. These will set the foundation for all that is to come when playing shred guitar. Your hands, wrists, and fingers must be in shape to execute the accelerated passages in this style of guitar playing.

12

Chapter II: Minor Pentatonic Scales

Lesson 6: Minor pentatonic scale pattern one

Now, when it comes to playing guitar solos and melody lines, the best place to start is the minor pentatonic scales. These are five scale patterns that span the fretboard. In this chapter, we will look at all five, starting with scale pattern one.

The reason why the pentatonic scales are so popular, both minor and major, is that they are easy to play, only use certain notes, and work with a wide variety of chord progressions and styles of music.

Pentatonic means a scale of five notes. Penta means five, and tonic means tones, or notes. And these five notes can be magical if you learn how to play them correctly.

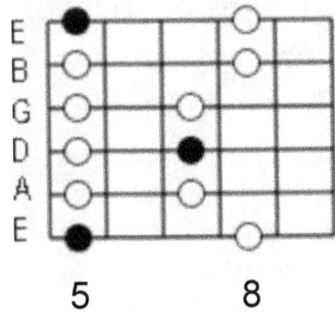

This is the A minor pentatonic scale. The most popular one on the planet. As you can see, it forms a box pattern. This allows for ease of use and understanding.

14

The reason why it is the A minor pentatonic is because of where it is located on the fretboard, and the fact that it uses certain notes that make it so.

If it is located in a different place on the fretboard, it will still be the pentatonic scale, but because the notes change, it will be in a different key. For instance, if we move the pentatonic scale to the 10th fret, it will now be the D minor pentatonic scale.

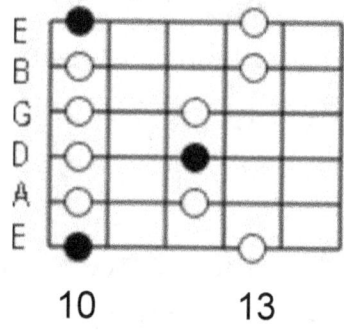

A wonderful thing about the guitar is the way it's designed. Notes change, but patterns stay the same. It takes out a lot of the guesswork. It's why it can be played by ear.

Let's look at this concept in more detail.

It all starts with the 12 notes of the musical alphabet.

A A# B C C# D D# E F F# G G#

Master these 12 notes as they are the foundation.

From the 12 notes that make up the musical alphabet, we take 7 to make the major scale. This is the Do Re Me Fa So La Ti Do that we are so familiar with. If you didn't study this in grammar school, I'm sure you've heard it before.

Anyway, the most common major scale to form out of the 12 notes is the C major scale. Why? Because it has no sharps or flats in it.

C major: C D E F G A B
1 2 3 4 5 6 7

If we add the C note at the end, we start ot go into the 2nd octave. So, when it comes to the Do Re Me, there are 8 with the 1st and 8th notes being the same. But technically, there are only 7 notes to the major scale.

If we want to make this into a minor scale, we need to alter a few notes. We need to flatten the 3rd, 6th, and 7th notes. By doing this, we will have created the C minor scale.

C major: C D E F G A B C = 1 2 3 4 5 6 7
C minor: C D Eb F G Ab Bb = 1 2 b3 4 5 b6 b7

Can you see how this works? By altering the 3 notes, we create a different scale. This is the basics of music theory.

The minor pentatonic scale is no different. It just uses fewer notes to make it more appealing to play.

A major: A B C# D E F# G# = 1 2 3 4 5   6   7
A minor: A B C D E F G = 1 2 b3 4 5 b6 b7

Notice how we flattened the same notes as in the C major scale to get the A minor scale? Now, if we want to make the A minor pentatonic scale, we need to use the 1 b3, 4, 5, and b7th notes.

A major: A B C# D E F# G# = 1 2 3 4 5 6 7
A minor: A B C D E F G = 1 2 b3 4 5 b6 b7
A minor pentatonic: A C D E G = 1 b3 4 5 b7

Do you see how we just took these five notes out of the A minor scale to create the A minor pentatonic scale? And the pattern makes the notes line up perfectly. No guesswork. Move it to a different position, and the notes change, but the pattern stays the same.

A minor pentatonic   C minor pentatonic

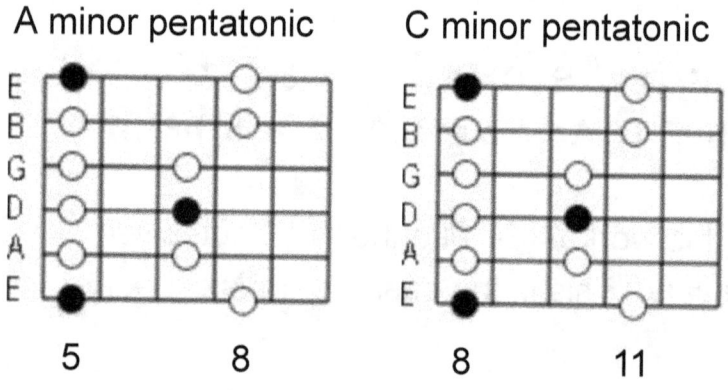

Lesson 7: Minor pentatonic scale pattern two

Now that we know a little bit about minor pentatonic scale pattern one, we will look at minor pentatonic scale pattern two. The reason why there are 5 patterns is that there are 5 notes to the pentatonic scale.

This allows us to play across the fretboard in different positions that use different frets, while still maintaining the same 5 notes. This gives us a road map along the fretboard in which to be more creative with the 5 notes in the pentatonic scale.

So in a sense, we are playing the same 5 notes, just doing them in different variations. And each scale pattern resides on each one of the notes in the pentatonic scale. Let's continue with the key of A minor as we did with pattern one.

A minor: A B C D E F G = 1 2 3 4 5 6 7
A minor pentatonic: A C D E G = 1 b3 4 5 b7

Since the pattern variations begin on each note, that tells us that pattern one will start on the A note, and pattern two will start on the C note.

Make sense?

Let's dive a little further.

What is great about these scale patterns is that they allow us to easily navigate the fretboard and break them down in such a way that they're easier to learn and understand.

Pentatonic scale pattern two:

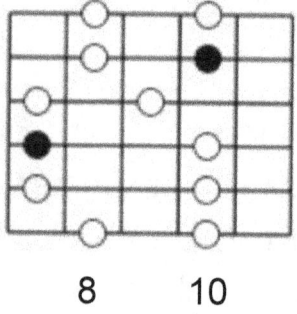

8   10

If you analyze the notes, you'll see that they are the same as pattern one. We just started on the C note instead of the A. Since the notes are in a different order, this gives us something new to create with. Kind of like a painter painting multiple Pictures with just five colors.

A minor pattern one = A C D E G
A minor pattern two = C D E G A

Can you see how we are using the same notes within the scale? We are just starting on the next one in line, the C note. In doing so, the notes line up in such a way that they give us a new pattern to work with.

Since we are still in the key of A minor, the pattern highlights where those notes are within the pentatonic scale pattern two. It is in two locations. On the 4th string, 7th fret, and on the 2nd string, 10th fret.

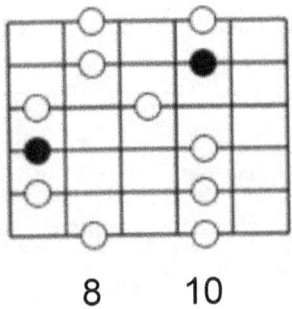

8   10

These are considered the root notes of the key you are playing in. That is why they are highlighted. They let you know you are in the same key even though you are playing in a different position on the fretboard.

A minor pattern one   A minor pattern two

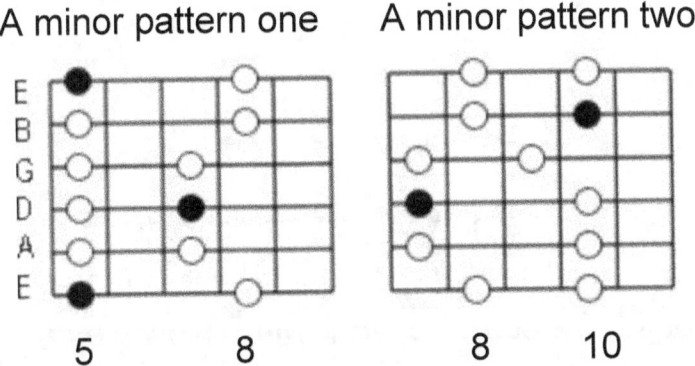

5   8   8   10

Pattern two will always be located after pattern one.

Lesson 8: Minor pentatonic pattern three

Now that we have scale patterns one and two down, we can take a look at pattern number three. The minor pentatonic scale pattern will start on the 3rd note in the scale. This note in the A minor pentatonic scale is D.

Since pattern one started on the 1st tone degree, and the second pattern started on the 3rd tone degree, it only makes sense that scale pattern three would start on the 4th tone degree.

A minor scale pattern three

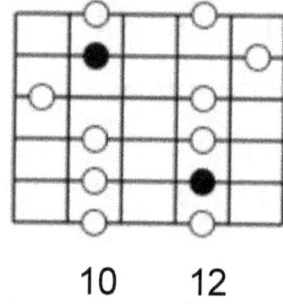

10   12

Here, we can see that we have a new variety of notes to work with. This not only allows us to expand our creativity, but also gives us more of the guitar fretboard to work with. Now we can move from the 5th fret up to the 12th fret.

Once again, if we look at the notes, we can see very clearly that we are starting on the 3rd tone degree, and just like scale pattern 2, we use the same notes.

A minor pattern one = A C D E G
A minor pattern two = C D E G A
A minor pattern three = D E G A C

This is what makes these scale patterns so wonderful and popular to use. They line up very nicely along the fretboard, and they connect in such a way that you can use them as a road map to stay in key.

How cool is that?

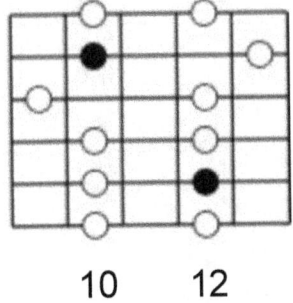

10   12

Just like with the other two scale patterns, the notes line up in such a way that we have another pattern to work with. The 10th fret is the D note, the 12th fret is the E note, and so forth.

So, when you think about it, if you know your notes on the fretboard and you know the notes within the scale, you can figure out the pattern easily. Just follow the notes, and unlock the mystery.

Since this is the third position of the minor scale, which starts on the 3rd note of the scale, you can see it gives a different pattern to work with, which gives us more diversity to create with. And like the other two, it stays the same in any key.

A minor Pentatonic = A C D E G = 1 b3 4 5 b7
G minor Pentatonic = G Bb C D F = 1 b3 4 5 b7

Pattern 3 in A minor   Pattern 3 G minor

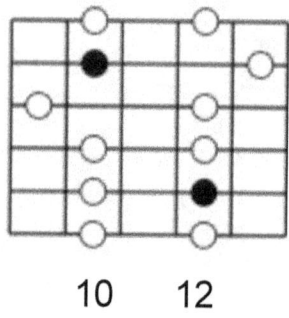   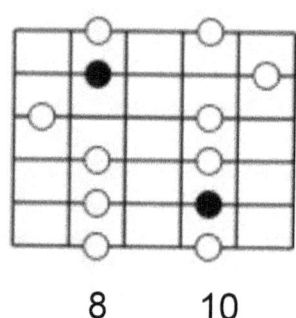

   10   12   8   10

In the key of G minor, the 5 notes needed to create the minor pentatonic scale would be the notes mentioned above. We look at the 3rd note (just like in A minor), and we can see that it is where pattern 3 is located. On the 8th fret of the 6th string.

This also tells us where pattern two would be played.

That is correct, on the B flat note at the 6th fret on the 6th string. And of course, pattern one in G minor would be played at the 3rd fret where the G note is located.

Make sense?

Remember, music is a language, and not only are you learning to shred on the guitar, but you're also learning a new language. Never forget this, because it is going to boost you above guitar players who just learn to play by ear.

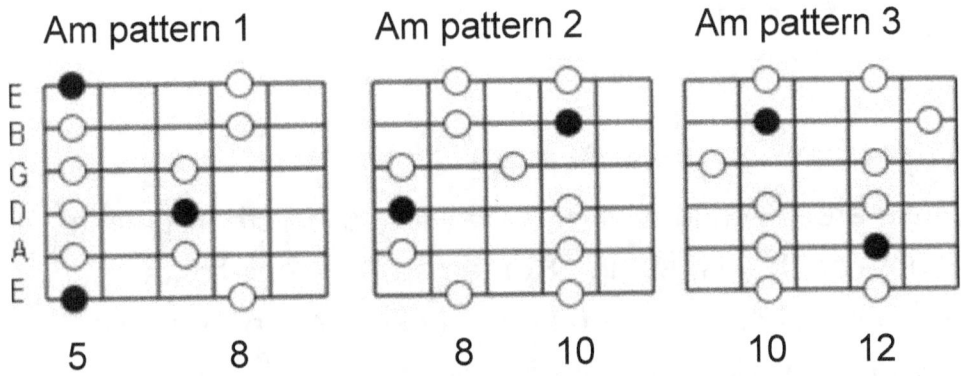

If you look at these three patterns, you can see how they just move up the fretboard in a certain sequence of frets. These are located on the notes of the A minor pentatonic scale.

Pattern 1 starts at the A note, pattern 2 starts at the C note, and pattern 3 starts at the D note. So, by clearly understanding this, we already know where the other 2 patterns are going to start, right? On the E and G notes of the scale.

24

Lesson 9: Minor pentatonic pattern four

Now we come to the 4th pattern of the minor pentatonic scale.
And like we learned in the last lesson, this one will start on the
4th note of the scale. Remember, this goes for any minor scale
we choose to play it in.

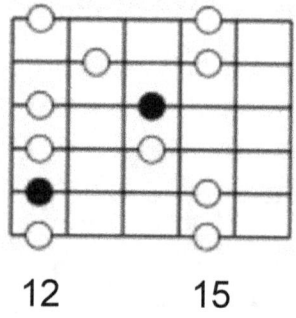

12   15

Since we are in A minor, we will play it at the 12th fret, which is
the E note on the 6th string. Remember, the highlighted notes
in the diagram are the root notes. These are the A notes.
Notice how they do this every five notes.

A minor pentatonic scale = A C D E G = 1 b3 4 5 b7

A minor pattern one = A C D E G
A minor pattern two = C D E G A
A minor pattern three = D E G A C
A minor pattern four = E G A C D

See how we use the same five notes over and over again? And since we start each one on a different note, it changes the pattern sequence. What this does is allow us the expand our creativity on what we can do with them.

This will be learned more in later chapters of the training. But for now, just get these patterns down. Know them like the back of your hand.

As you learn these minor pentatonic patterns, go through them individually and see how they offer different ways that you can get from note to note. Look at them ike a road map that you travel on.

Remember, when you play this pattern in a different key, the pattern stays the same, but the notes change. No guesswork, this just happens automatically by design. So all we need to do is do two things:

1. **Master the pattern**
2. **Master where to play it in any given key**

Not too difficult to do, right? Of course, it's always easier said than done, but if you just take it one step at a time, it will eventually come to you, and you'll figure it out.

Now let's look at all 4 patterns in the key of A minor.

All four pentatonic patterns in A minor:

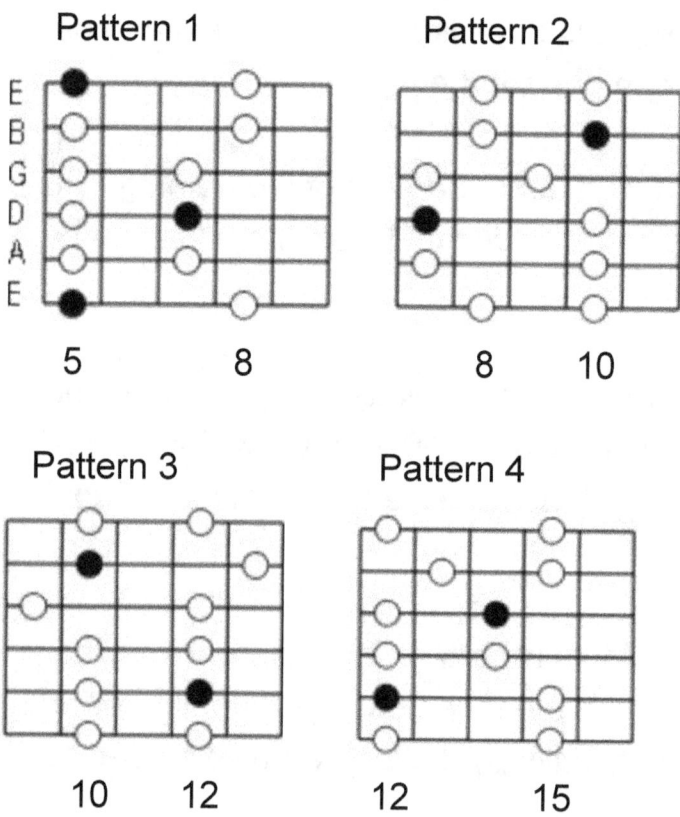

Notice how the A note (which is highlighted) changes position in each pattern. This is important to know because the root note is always a good place to jump off, or land on, when doing a guitar lick, or melody line.

If you know your notes along the fretboard on the 6th string, you'll also notice how these patterns are all formed from the notes that reside in the A minor scale.

Lesson 10: Minor pentatonic pattern five

Now we come to the last and final pattern, the fifth pattern. This pattern is cool because it's relatively easy to remember, and it can be played in two spots within the key of A minor.

Since we know that each pattern resides on a note of the minor pentatonic scale, then by now, you should now know what note this last pattern will start on.

Do you know?

That's right, it starts on the G note. What is great about this note is where it's located on the fretboard. It is located at the 15th fret, and also at the 3rd fret behind pattern one.

Pattern 5 (low)   Pattern 5 (high)

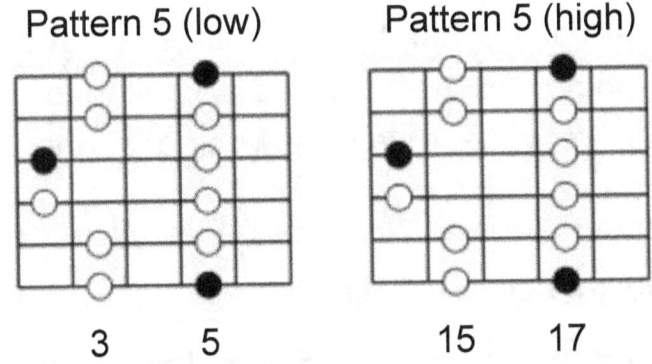

   3   5   15   17

Can you see how the pattern shape is the same in both positions?

28

Being that this is the case with this pattern, we can play it in both locations. By doing this, it gives us two things that the other patterns don't.

1. **It gives us the option for a low tone or a high tone**
2. **It gives us extended mastery over the fretboard**

If we play the 5th pattern at the 3rd fret, we are going to get a lower tone.

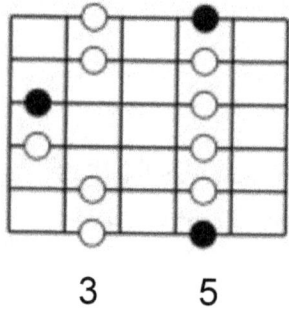

3   5

If we play this same pattern at the 15th fret, we will get a higher tone. This is beneficial to know as it will give us the option to create a guitar lick (which we will learn later how to do) in one position and move it to the next one.

This works because they are the same notes in both positions. This is a very common approach to lead guitar playing.

Now, let's look at all 5 pentatonic scale patterns in the key of A minor:

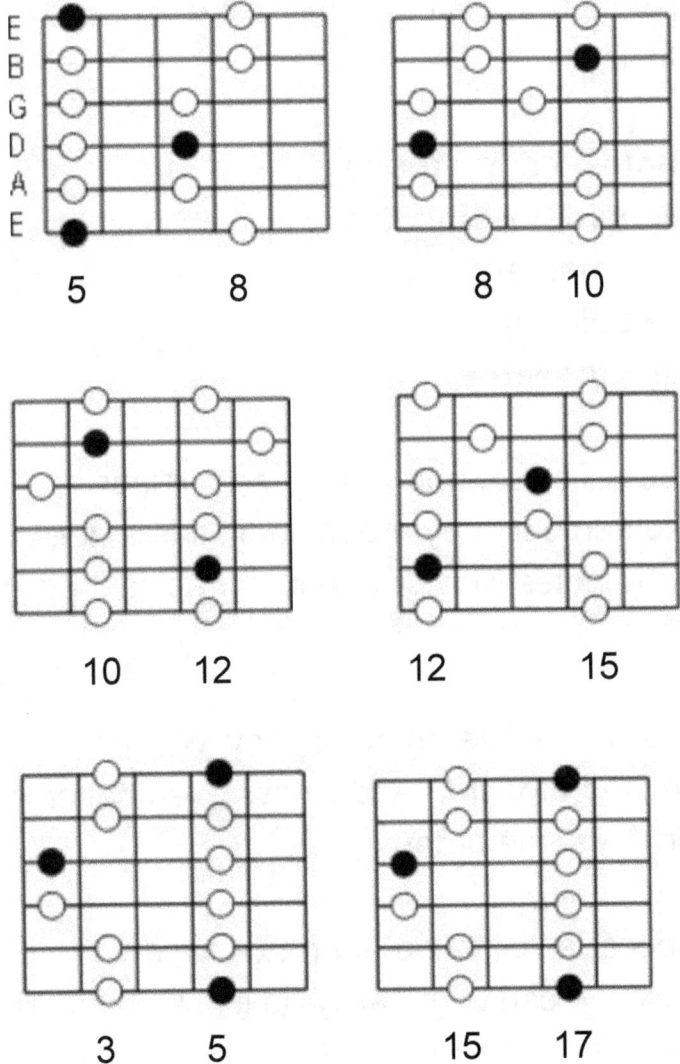

Pattern 5 is presented in both positions. The lower and the higher. Master these patterns and their location.

If you look closely at these five minor pentatonic patterns, they span from the A note on the 5th fret of the 6th string to the 17th fret of the 6th string. And if you master the interval of notes within them, you will have a road map that will allow you to accomplish a few cool things.

1. **Play the same notes 5 different ways**
2. **Create with unlimited possibilities**
3. **Develop fretboard mastery**
4. **Stay in key while soloing**
5. **Enhance your music theory**

All this and more can be accomplished with these 5 minor pentatonic patterns. Remember, they are minor in this order, because we are using the notes within the A minor scale they come out of.

If we want to change them to a different minor key, we just move them up or down the fretboard. And what's even better is that they always stay in the same order.

This is very beneficial because once we learn to navigate between them in A minor, we can then easily do it in G minor, B minor, D minor, E minor, etc.

Master these 5 minor pentatonic scale patterns, and develop a solid foundation for lead guitar shredding.

Chapter II Summary

First, we learned about minor pentatonic scale pattern one. This is the most common scale pattern and usually the first one everyone learns.

Second, we examine the second minor pentatonic scale pattern. This one will start where pattern one leaves off. By knowing this pattern, you can expand where you play along the fretboard.

Third, we then examine pattern three of the minor pentatonic scales. This is a great selection of notes because it allows you to not only expand the fretboard as pattern two does, but also gives you more options to work with.

Fourth, we then examine pentatonic scale pattern four. Once again, this not only allows you to expand the use of the fretboard, but it also develops more options for your lead guitar playing.

Lastly, we learn about the fifth pentatonic scale pattern. What is great about this pattern is that it is easy to execute and brings you back to square one. By learning all five patterns, you span the whole fretboard, which is essential for lead guitar shredding.

32

Chapter III: Major Pentatonic Scales

Lesson 11: Major Pentatonic pattern one

Now we come to the major pentatonic scale patterns. These have five of them, too. Why? Remember what I taught you about the pentatonic scale, meaning a scale of five notes. Well, the major pentatonic scale has five notes too.

But, since we are in a major key, we will not use a flat 3rd or a flat 7th note. We will choose different notes out of the major key to create the major pentatonic scale. Still five notes, but these will be different than the minor.

Let's take a closer look.

C major scale: C D E F G A B = 1 2 3 4 5 6 7
C major pentatonic scale: C D E G A = 1 2 3 5 6

To create the major pentatonic scale, we will not use the 1st, 2nd, 3rd, 5th, and 6th notes. We will leave out the 4th and the 7th. This will give us a different sound than the minor. This will provide more of an uplifting sound, as major usually does.

So, what patterns do we use for the major pentatonic? Well, let's take a look a the notes.

Since we are using the C major scale (any major scale will do; this one is just easiest), we need to look at the notes again.

C major: C D E F G A B C
C major pentatonic: C D E G A

We can see that we need a pattern that has two things;

1. **Uses the five notes above**
2. **Has the C and D notes on the 6th string**

The scale pattern that has these criteria is the pentatonic scale pattern two.

Major pentatonic pattern 1

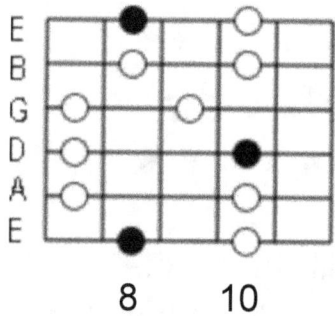

8   10

If you go through the notes of this pattern starting on the C note at the 8th fret, you will see very clearly that it uses the notes mentioned above. C, D, E, G, A

So we can concur that this is the major pentatonic scale. And, if we play it anywhere else, like say for instance, the 3rd fret, it will still be the major pentatonic scale. Play it at the 3rd fret it becomes the G major pentatonic scale.

Let's look at this in more detail:

G major scale: G A B C D E F# = 1 2 3 4 5 6 7
G major pentatonic scale: G A B D E = 1 2 3 5 6

G major pentatonic scale

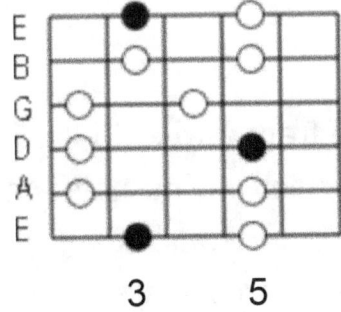

If you go through this scale pattern, you will see that the notes line up perfectly. That is what makes these pentatonic scale patterns so cool: the notes change automatically even though the patterns stay the same!

Like the minor pentatonic scales, this takes out the guesswork and works in any major key. This allows you to focus more on shredding awesome guitar solos.

Now let's see if this works in the key of A major:

A major scale: A B C# D E F# G# = 1 2 3 4 5 6 7
A major pentatonic scale: A B C# E F# = 1 2 3 5 6

A major pentatonic pattern one

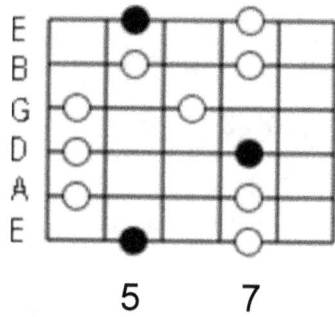

Once again, if you look at your notes on the fretboard or in this scale, you can see that the notes line up perfectly! The notes in this pattern are the notes within the A major pentatonic scale. Just like they were in the C and G major pentatonic scales.

So, if you decide to play a shredding guitar solo in a major key, no matter which one it is, you can play this pentatonic scale pattern in the first position, and it will sound great!

Well, that is if you practice and learn to use it properly.

Now, since this is major pentatonic scale pattern one, then the next pattern will be major pentatonic scale pattern two, and so forth and so forth.

Lesson 12: Major pentatonic pattern two

Now we come to major pentatonic pattern two. Since pattern two is now in the 1st position and the pentatonic patterns are always in the same order, that tells us what the second pentatonic pattern is.

C Major pentatonic pattern two

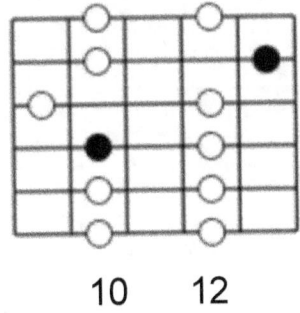

10   12

If we stick with the C major scale, we can see once again that the second pattern starts on the second note of the C major pentatonic scale, and the notes line up as they should.

C major pattern one: C D E G A
C major pattern two: D E G A C

The same thing goes for the other keys that we looked at. Once you know the notes within the key (any major key), you can find exactly where the patterns are located along the fretboard.

If we play in the key of A major and want to play in A major pentatonic pattern 2, we play it at the next note in the scale.

A major pentatonic scale: A B C# E F#

From what we see in this scale, we can tell that major pentatonic pattern two starts at the B note. Because this is the 2nd note in the scale.

A major pentatonic pattern 2

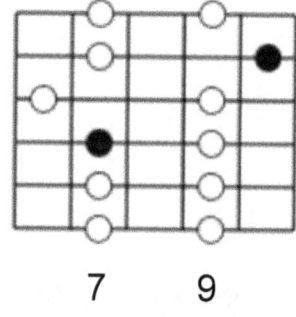

7   9

A major pattern one: A B C# E F#
A major pattern two: B C# E F# A

Can you see that if we play it here at the 2nd note location within the scale, the notes change and line up perfectly, like in the previous key?

This is the magic of the fretboard and how the notes upon it can be broken down into simple patterns that can give us a nice, comprehensive way to manage them.

Lesson 13: Major pentatonic pattern three

Now that we know major pentatonic patterns one and two, we can work on pattern three. Of course, from learning the minor pentatonic scale patterns, we already know this one. It's just a matter of where to play it.

Let's say we play it in the key of C major. Where will it be located on the fretboard? Let's take a look.

C major pentatonic: C D E G A
C major pattern three: E G A C D

Since pattern three starts on the 3rd note of the scale, we know that it is the E note, and this is located at the 12th fret. So this is where this third major pattern would be played.

Do the notes line up? Let's take a look.

C major pentatonic pattern three

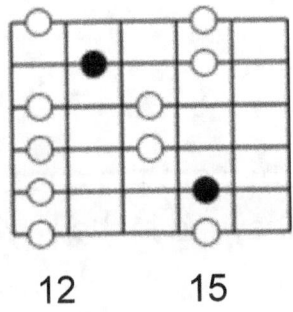

12   15

If the E note is at the 12th fret, then the next note at the 15th fret would be the G. The note at the 12th fret on the 5th string is the A note, the note on the 15th fret 5th string is the C note, and the note at the 12th fret 4th string is the D note.

So it looks like the note does up within the scale just like the other two major pentatonic patterns. Now, does it work with other keys? Let's take a look.

A major pentatonic: A B C# E F#
A major pentatonic pattern three: C# E F# A B

The notes above tell us we need to play this pattern on the C# note. This is located at the 9th fret on the 6th string.

A major pentatonic pattern three

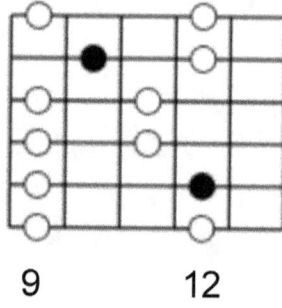

9   12

If you look these notes over, you will see that they are the ones in the scale. They line up in this key just like they did in the key of C major. And this goes for all major keys.

Lesson 14: Major pentatonic pattern four

Now we come to major petatonic pattern four. And once again, just like the other three, we start at the 4th note in the scale. If we stay with the key of C major, what note would it be? Do you remember? If not, let's take a look.

C major pentatonic scale: C D E G A

According to the notes above, the 4th note in the scale is the G note. So this is where we will play the 4th pattern of the C major pentatonic scale. Sometimes these are called positions, but I like to call them patterns because they change shape.

Major pentatonic pattern four

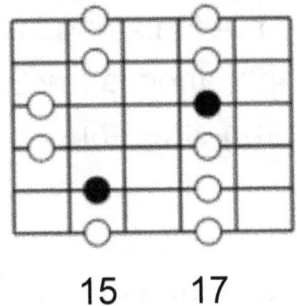

15   17

Now that we know the pattern and where it is located, we want to make sure we are correct. Well, this will happen if the notes line up correctly. That's how you know if what you are playing is correct.

C major pentatonic scale: C D E G A
C major pattern four: G A C D E

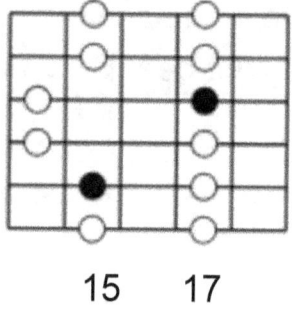

15   17

Let's see: The note at the 15th fret on the 6th string is the G note, the note at the 17th fret on the 6th string is the A note, and the note on the 5th fret on the 5th string is the C note. We know this is the C note because it is highlighted.

When we continue, the note at the 17th fret on the 5th string is a D note, and the note on the 14th fret on the 4th string is the E note. See, the notes line up perfectly, just like the other three major pentatonic patterns do.

This is how we know we are on the right track and the patterns will fit like they're supposed to when we shred a solo in the key of C major.

Do the same thing with the other keys that I mentioned in the previous lessons. Find where this 4th pattern will be located in the key of A major and G major for fretboard mastery.

Lesson 15: Major pentatonic pattern five

Now we come to the 5th and final major pentatonic scale pattern. Major pentatonic pattern five. This will be located at the 5th note in the key it comes out of. If we stick with the key of C major, this will be at the A note.

Why? Because A is the 5th note in the C major pentatonic scale.

C major pentatonic scale: C D E G A
C Major pentatonic pattern five: A C D E G

Remember, when playing all these scale patterns, we use the same 5 notes; we just start on a different one for each pattern. And it is this, starting on a different note, that gives us more variety within the scale.

C major pentatonic pattern five

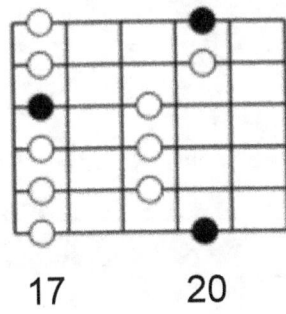

17   20

44

Once again, just like with the other four major pentatonic scale patterns, the notes line up as they should. If you go through them, you will see that they do. Do they line up with other major pentatonic scales? They should.

Let's take a look.

D major scale: D E F# G A B C# = 1 2 3 4 5 6 7
D major pentatonic: D E F# A B = 1 2 3 5 6

According to the notes above, the 5th D major pentatonic pattern would be based on the B note, and it should line up as it did in C major. The five notes in D are B, D, E, F#, and A.

Now, we know the pattern as it is the same as the one in C major; we just need to know where to play it. According to our musical knowledge, it should be played at the B note.

This can be either done at the 7th or 19th fret on the 6th string.

D major pentatonic pattern 5 in both places

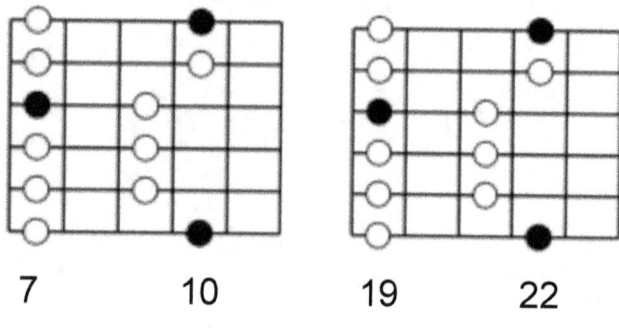

7   10   19   22

Now, let's look at the notes and see if we are correct in the placement of D major pentatonic pattern 5. Since we are starting on the 5th note, the B note, and the notes go in a specific order, they should line up.

Let's see if we are correct.

D major pentatonic pattern five: B D E F# A

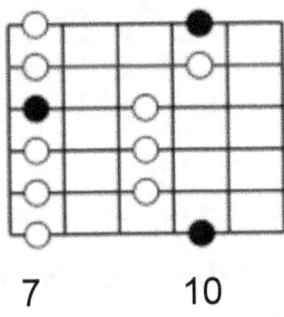

7   10

Ok, the 7th fret on the 6th string is the B note, the 10th fret on the 6th string is the D note, the 7th fret on the 5th string is the E note, the 9th fret on the 5th string is the F# note, and the 7th fret on the 4th string is the A note.

So yes, they do line up. Can you see how cool this is? Can you see that if you play these patterns in the correct order and the correct place within any major key, they'll work?

Can you also see that the same five patterns work for both major and minor? Just know which one and where to play it.

Chapter III summary

First, we learned that there are also five major pentatonic scales. In the first part of Chapter Three, we examine major pentatonic scale pattern one.

Second, we learn about major pentatonic scale pattern two. Once again, this allows us to expand the fretboard. It also allows you to play over major chord progressions in any key you choose.

Third, we learn about major pentatonic scale pattern three. This starts where pattern two leaves off, giving you the chance to expand along the fretboard. The more you do this, the better you get to know the notes within the scale.

Fourth, we look at the fourth major pentatonic scale pattern. Once again, this pattern starts where the previous pattern left off. Very much like connecting puzzle pieces. A great way to expand along the fretboard.

Lastly, we look at major pentatonic scale pattern 5. This leads us back to pattern one, just like with the minor pentatonic scale patterns. These patterns are interlocking in both major and minor keys. It is just where you play them that matters.

Chapter IV: Adding The Blue Note

Lesson 16: Minor blues scale pattern one

What is the blue note? Well, I'm glad you asked. It is when we add a note to the scales that we have already learned, to give them a darker, moodier sound.

Very common in rock, blues, and jazz music. The perfect type of emotion for shredding on the guitar. In these examples, we will work with the minor pentatonic scale.

To create this emotion, we add a note to the pentatonic scale and turn it into the blues scale. This allows us to expand our scale vocabulary for a wider range of improvisation and melodic expressive possibilities.

The note that we will be adding will be the flat 5th note.

A minor pentatonic: A C D E G = 1 b3 4 5 b7
A minor blues scale: A C D Eb E G = 1 b3 4 b5 5 b7

If we look at this example, we can see that to make the blues scale, we add the flat 5th note. In the case of A minor, this note is E flat.

Since we already know the minor pentatonic scale, this will be easy. We just need to find the fourth and play the note after it. So, the note we're adding will be between the fourth and fifth notes. In the minor pentatonic, we can find it in two places.

A minor blues scale

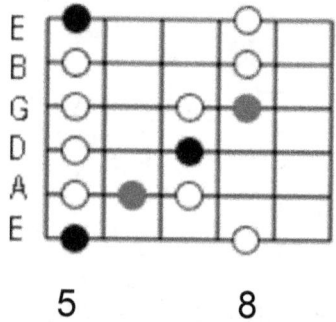

If you look closely at the diagram above, you can see that the flat fifth note, or the bue note as it is called, is located at the 6th fret on the 5th string and also at the 8th fret on the 3rd string.

Knowing this allows for a few things.

1. **Expands our improvisational possibilities**
2. **Expands our scale vocabulary**
3. **Adds emotional depth**

These things and more can be benefited from knowing the minor blues scale. Enabling you to express yourself more fully and creatively. With a fuller understanding of music theory.

The blues scale works in all minor keys just like the minor pentatonic. Can you see how they are closely related and how you can add emotion to the minor pentatonic scale by adding the blue note?

Let's see how this works in the key of G minor.

G minor pentatonic scale: G Bb C D F = 1 b3 4 5 b7
G minor blues scale: G Bb C Db D F = 1 b3 4 b5 5 b7

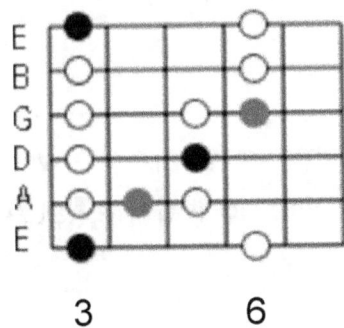

We can see that the blue note (flat 5th) is in the same two locations in this key as it was in A minor. Once again, the pattern stays the same, but the notes change.

If you review the notes, you will see that this added note is the flat D note in these two locations.

Let's try this out in other minor keys along the fretboard, and when reviewing the notes, you'll see they line up perfectly.

50

Let's look at the D minor pentatonic scale.

D minor pentatonic scale: D F G A C = 1 b3 4 5 b7
D minor blues scale: D F G Ab A C = 1 b3 4 b5 5 b7

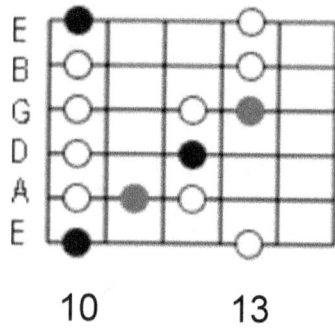

10   13

Since the D note is located at the 10th fret, this is where we will play this scale. Now, do the notes line up? We added the flat A note. Is it located where it should be?

Yes, it does. The note that is on the 11th fret on the 5th string is the A flat note. The flat 5th note that we added to the D minor pentatonic scale. It is also located at the 13th fret on the 3rd string.

Can you see how this works? Once you learn and master the minor pentatonic scales, adding the blue note will be easy, as long as you know where to add it in the two places.

Master where you will add the blue note to pattern one.

Lesson 17: Minor blues scale pattern two

This same thing can be done with the 2nd minor pentatonic pattern. We just find where the 4th and 5th notes are, and we add a note between them.

A minor pentatonic pattern two: C D E G A
A minor blues scale pattern two: C D Eb E G A

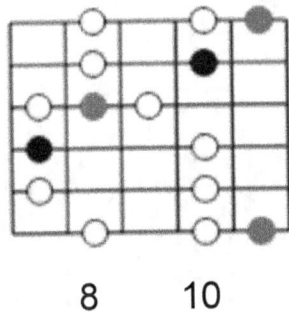

8   10

Remember, this 2nd pattern shape will start on the 2nd note of the pentatonic scale. In A minor key, this is the C note. Since this is the case, the note will be added in this pattern, which will be the E flat note.

You can see that in pattern two, it is added in three different locations. At the 11th fret on the 6th string, at the 8th fret on the 3rd string, and at the 11th fret on the 1st string. These three locations help us expand this pattern.

This concept works in other minor keys as well. We just moved the scale to different locations along the fretboard. And remember, to find the second note in the scale, locate where the scale is played, and proceed from there.

G minor pentatonic pattern two: Bb C D F G
G blues scale pattern two: Bb C Db D F G

In this example, we are adding the D flat note, and we are playing this second minor blues pattern on the 6th fret because that is where the B flat note is located.

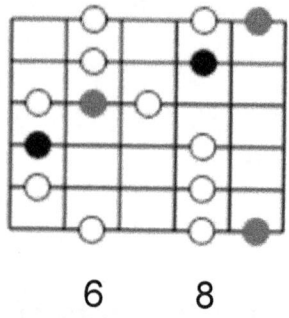

6   8

Do the notes line up? Let's take a look. The note we are looking at adding is the E-flat note. Well, it seems like it is, and it is located at the same three places it was in A minor.

The 9th fret on the 6th string, the 6th fret on the 3rd string, and the 9th fret on the 1st string. See what makes these scale patterns so powerful?

Lesson 18: Minor blues scale pattern three

We can do the same thing with the third minor pentatonic scale pattern. If we are in the key of A minor, what is the 3rd note? That's right, the D note.

A minor pentatonic scale: A C D E G
A minor pentatonic scale pattern three: D E G A C
A minor blues scale pattern three: D Eb E G A C

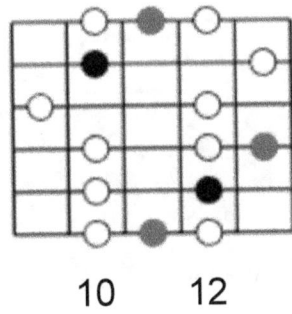

10   12

Once again, in the key of A minor, we add the E-flat note to pattern three in 3 locations. Just like we did in pattern two. This allows us to expand the pattern and enhance our improvisational creativity.

And just like the previous two patterns, we can use this in other keys in the same way. We just need to know the key we are playing in and where this scale pattern is located.

54

What if we want to play in the key of G minor? Where would this scale pattern be located?

Well, let's take a look.

G minor pentatonic scale: G Bb C D F
G minor pentatonic pattern three: C D F G Bb
G blues scale pattern three: C Db D F G Bb

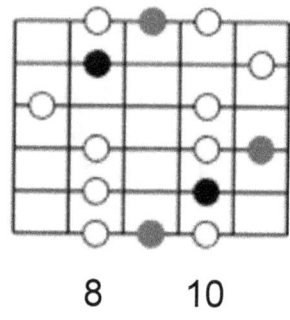

8   10

Once again, just like with the key of A minor, if we play this blues scale in the proper location, the notes line up perfectly.

We start on the 3rd note of the scale, which is C, and it is located at the 8th fret on the 6th string. The scale above tells us that the blue note or flat 5th is the D flat. Which is located at the 9th fret on the 6th string.

And, just like the pattern in A minor, it is located in 3 places. So with that being the case, we don't need to think about it. We just need to play it, bitsause we know it lines up like it should.

That is what's great about playing the guitar. Once you realize how this works, you unlock the mystery of the notes. You then realize that all you have to do is know where to move along the fretboard in any given key, and you've got it.

As long as you play the correct pattern in the right location, the notes will magically line up, and what you play will be in key. No need for second-guessing.

This is the problem that most guitar players face when starting to learn to play guitar solos. Staying in key. They learn a pattern or two, and as long as they stay within those two patterns, they're fine.

But if they step outside of them, ouch! Bad notes start happening, and people start cringing from hearing music that is not in harmony.

But this won't happen to you if you master what is being taught in this training. If you learn these scale patterns and master where to play them, the options are limitless for what you can do with them.

Should we look at this pattern in one more key?

Why not. Let's take a look at blues pattern 3 in one more key. How about the key of D minor?

We looked at the key of D minor earlier, so this should be easy. I like the key of D minor because it's further away from A minor, which is the most common key to learn the minor pentatonic scales in.

Remember, the blues scale is just the minor pentatonic scale with the flat 5th note added. And it is this magic note that gives it its character.

D minor pentatonic scale: D F G A C
D minor pentatonic pattern three: G A C D F
D minor blues scale: G Ab A C D F

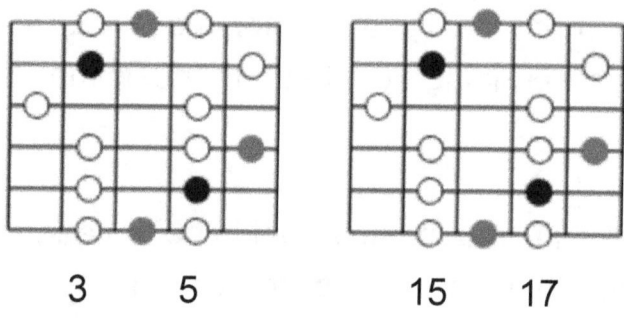

If we look at the notes, they line up within the pattern as they should, that is, if we play it in these two locations. Remember, since we're playing the 3rd blues scale pattern, we start on the 3rd note, which is G.

Try this with other keys, and see how it magically works.

Lesson 19: Minor blues scale pattern four

Now, we come to pattern four of the blues scale. Where is this going to start? That's right, on the 4th note of the scale, just like we did with the other ones.

If we start with A minor, we are going to look for the 4th note within the scale to find where to play this scale pattern. Of course, by now, this should be relatively easy because we know it's just A minor pentatonic pattern 4 with the blue note added.

A minor pentatonic scale: A C D E G
A minor pentatonic pattern four: E G A C D
A minor blues scale pattern four: E G A C D Eb

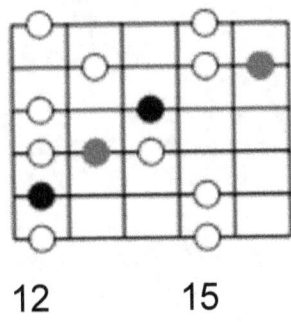

12   15

Look at this pattern, can you see the notes line up?

58

That is, if we play it here at the 12th fret. If we were to play it at the 9th fret, the notes wouldn't line up for the key of A minor. But they would line up for a different key. Do you happen to know what key that would be?

Minor blues pattern 4 at the 9th fret. What key would this be in? See if you can figure this out. If not, reach out, and I'll give you the answer.

What if we play this pattern in G minor, like we did with the third pattern? Where would it be located?

G minor pentatonic scale: G Bb C D F
G minor pentatonic pattern four: D F G Bb C
G blues scale pattern four: D F G Bb C Db

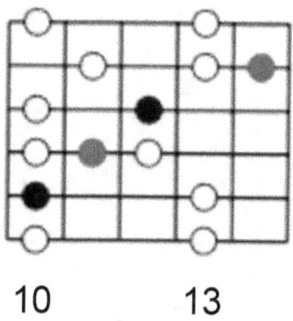

10   13

Once again, if we play this in the correct place along the fretboard, we discover that the notes line up perfectly. All of them. The only difference is that the blue note is located in only two places in this scale pattern. Try this out with other keys.

Lesson 20: Minor blues scale pattern five

Now we come to the 5th and final minor blues scale pattern. This pattern will be the 5th minor pentatonic scale pattern, with the flat 5th note added. Just like the other 4 blues patterns.

Staying with the key of A minor to start, let's see where this blue note will reside within the 5th minor pentatonic pattern.

A minor pentatonic: A C D E G
A minor pentatonic pattern five: G A C D E
A minor blues pattern five G A C D Eb E

Remember, pattern 5 is going to start on the 5th note of the scale. In this case, it will be the G note. And this note is located at the 3rd fret, as well as the 15th. Like before, this gives us two handy places to play it.

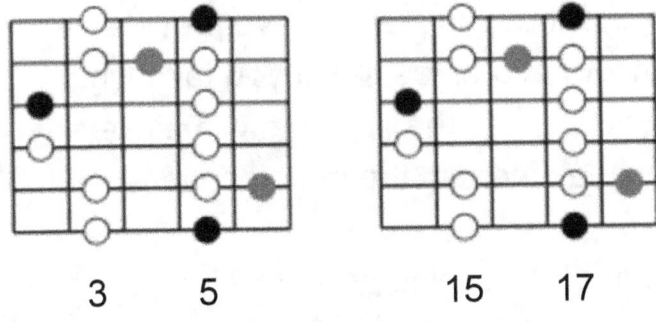

3   5   15   17

Do you see how the notes line up in both locations?

Let's look at this in more detail.

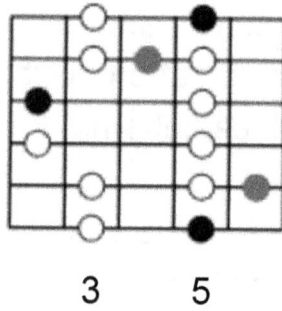

3   5

We start on the G note at the 3rd fret on the 6th string. The A note follows on the 5th fret of the 6th string, the C note is on the 3rd fret of the 5th string, the D note is on the 5th fret of the 5th string, and the Eb note is on the 6th fret of the 5th string.

Which would make the final note, the E note, at the 2nd fret on the 4th string. If you look at the notes at the 15th fret when playing the pattern there, you will see that they are the same.

Try this out with all the keys that you play in. I've provided a few here in these lessons for examples, but if you take what you've learned further, you will see that it works wth all keys. That is provided that you play them in the right locations.

And, you can create major blues scales as well. Use the same concept, but instead of adding the flat 5th note to the major pentatonic scale, you'll add the flat 3rd note. This will widen your perspective even more.

Chapter IV Summary

First, we have learned that there is an additional note that we can add to the pentatonic scales, and it is called the blue note. This note adds a dark, bluesy mood to the scale.

Second, we then look at what note this is. In the minor pentatonic scale, it will be the flat 5th note. So, now instead of the scale being made up of five notes, it will be made up of six notes.

Third, we learn that this flat fifth note is located in each scale pattern and where it is located. By knowing this, you can skip over it to create the mood of the scale or add it to darken the mood of the scale.

Fourth, we learn that this flat fifth note is located in the fourth minor pentatonic scale. We look at the difference between the minor pentatonic scale, pattern four, and the blues scale, pattern four.

Lastly, we learn where this note is located in pattern five of the minor pentatonic scale. Remember, these scale patterns start on the five notes of the scale they are derived from. Knowing this will allow you to unlock the mysteries of the fretboard.

62

Chapter V: Personality Traits

Lesson 21: Hammer-ons and pull-offs

Now that we know how to form the scales and where to play them, it is time to learn how to bring them to life. This is done with personality traits. The two most common are hammer-ons and pull-offs.

These are two techniques that add and subtract notes. A hammer-on allows you to pick a note, and then hammer-on to the next one without picking it. A pull-off is the opposite. You pick a note and pull off to the one behind it.

The first one we'll look at will be the hammer-on. This technique is indicated in the tab by an arc above both notes. This will build finger strength and endurance.

Hammer-on: adding a note

Pick the note on the 5th fret, 3rd string, and hammer-on to the 7th fret without picking the note.

Pull-off: subtracting a note

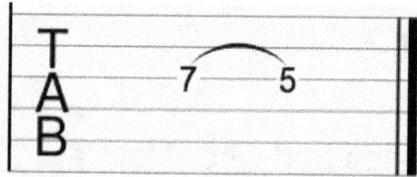

Place two fingers on the 7th and 5th frets. Pick the 7th fret and pull off from the 7th back to the note on the 5th fret. You should hear two notes in both the hammer-on and pull-off examples.

Both of these techniques are indicated by an arc above both notes. The way you know which is which is by the numbers. With a hammer-on, the note gets larger. With a pull-off, the number gets smaller. Watch for this as you read the tabs.

Hammer-on pull-off: adding them together

Here we have a hammer-on pull-off from the 5th fret to the 7th, back to the 5th. This is also a very common way to play these two techniques. Play them within the scales you've learned and listen to how they sound.

Lesson 22: Slides and string bends

The next guitar licks that we will learn are the slides and string bends. These two techniques are another great way to express the notes within the scales. Remember, guitar licks are tools used to make the scales sound like music.

Let's start with the slide. This can be done both up the fretboard as well as down. And will be indicated in the tab as a diagonal line between the two notes.

Slides: up and back down

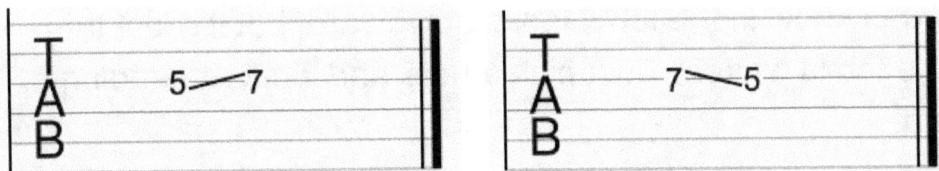

You pick the note at the 5th fret, 3rd string, and slide up to the 7th. You then pick the note at the 7th fret and slide back down to the 5th fret. Only pick the 1st note.

Notice that the direction of the diagonal line changes. Remember, sliding down is toward the headstock, and sliding up is toward the bridge. Try this out with notes in the scales and hear how they sound.

Now we come to the string bend. This is where you pick a note and bend it up. This can be bent up to the note on the next fret, or two frets up.

String bends: pick the note and bend it up.

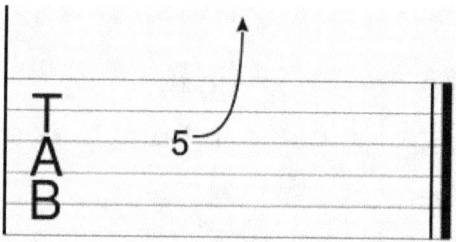

You pick the note at the 5th fret on the 3rd string and push it upward. I know in the tab it looks downward, but it's just the way the tab is written. Just pick a note and work at bending it upward.

Bend & release: Bend and release for two notes

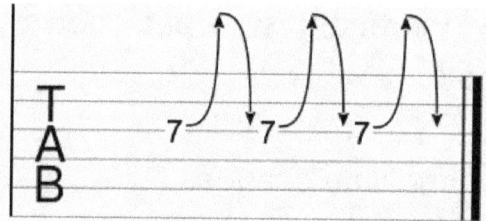

You can also bend the string and release it to create two notes. Try this with notes on the scale, and listen to how they sound.

Lesson 23: Trills and vibrato

Now we come to a couple of techniques that have interesting names. Trills and vibrato. A trill is when you do a repeated hammer-on pull-off, and vibrato is when you pick a note and vibrate it slightly up and down.

The trill builds off the hammer-on pull-off technique learned earlier. We just repeat it a few times. Once you learn this, you'll begin to hear it in solos of your favorite players.

Trill: repeated hammer-on pull-off

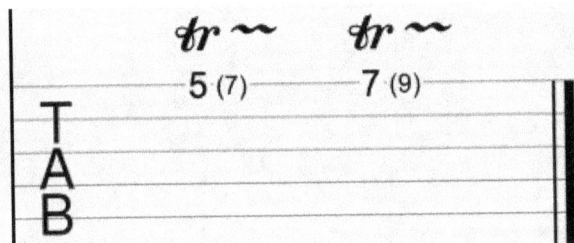

Here you pick the notes at the 5th and 7th frets, and trill onto the 7th and 9th frets. A trill is indicated in the tab by a tr and followed by a wavy line.

Now we come to the awesome technique called vibrato. This is where you pick a note on any string and gently vibrate it. This is done by rotating the wrist of the finger that is pressing on the string.

Vibrato is a great technique because it adds a singing quality to the note. Very much like a singer does with their voice when they hold a note and vibrate their vocal cords.

This is the same kind of effect you are trying to achieve.

Vibrato: pick the string and vibrate it

Here, you pick the note at the 7th fret on the 3rd string and vibrate the note up and down. Vibrato is indicated by a wavy line above the number.

This technique develops differently for every player, and as time goes on, you'll develop your vibrato. That is, if you work on it daily. Vibrato is very common in guitar solos, so make sure to do so. As it will be well worth the effort.

Lesson 24: Triplets and melodic shapes

Another couple of cool things you can do to make the scales sound cool are triplets and melodic shapes. These are a sequence of notes played in a pattern.

Triplets are a sequence of three notes that are repeated, and melodic shapes can be moved up and down the fretboard as they are repeated.

Triplets: three notes that are repeated.

Here we have a triplet that uses the infamous hammer-on at the 5th fret 2nd string, and finishes at the 5th fret 1st string. We also have a double dotted line at the end of the measure that lets us know to repeat the triplets.

Many cool sounds can be done with triplets, and as you learn to play them, you'll hear how they are used in many of your favorite guitar solos.

70

Melodic shapes:

These are patterns of notes that are taken out of scales. These can be moved up and down the fretboard to create melodic landscapes of color. They allow you to create melodies that fit harmonically into a chord progression.

Notes from scales and chords can be used to create melodic shapes that add flair to your guitar solos.

Melodic shapes along the E string:

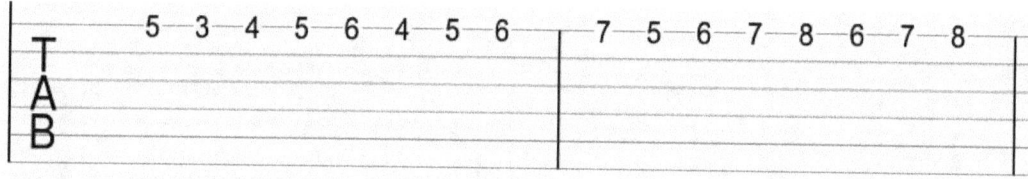

In this example, we have a shape of notes that go up the fretboard along the high E string. From the 5th fret to the 8th.

```
      5  4  5  6  5  6  7  6    7  8  7  8  9  8  9  10
T
A
B
```

This example is very similar, but goes from the 5th fret up to the 10th. Practice these daily for the best results.

Lesson 25: Alternate and tremolo picking

When it comes to speed and accuracy, you need to learn to do alternate and tremolo picking. These two things are what emphasize the name guitar shredding.

Alternate picking:
This is where you pick down on the string, and then back up.

Example #1: On the sixth string

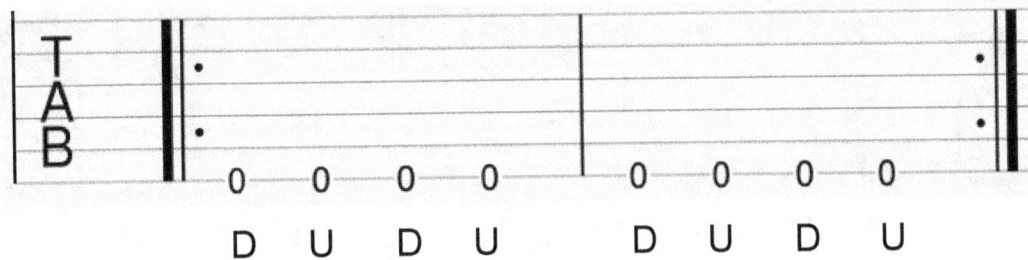

Example #2: With the open E chord

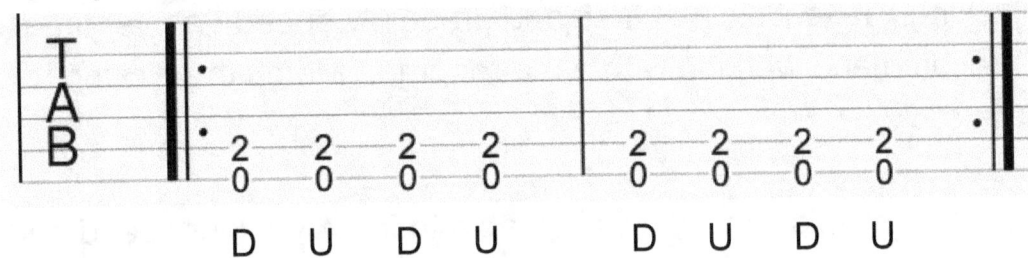

Example 1 alternate picks on the 6th string, and example 2 does the same thing, except you hold the open E chord while doing it. Practice this slowly at first to get it down.

Alternate picking continued:

Example #3: On the first string

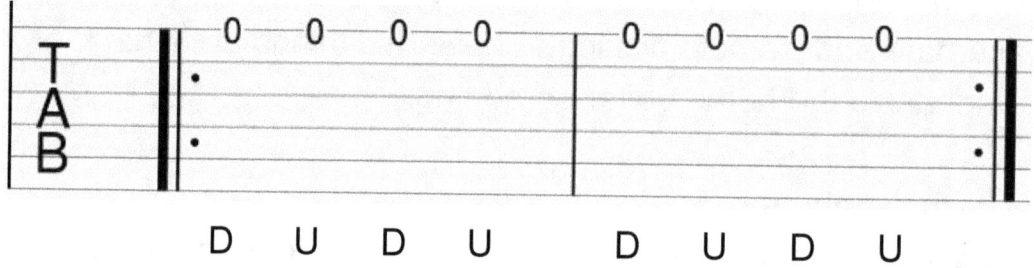

Example #4: On the 12th fret

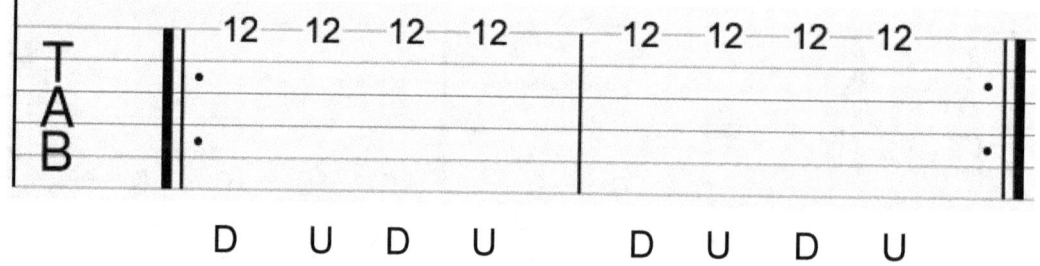

All 4 of these examples will give you a great start into alternate picking. Take it slow at first, and gradually speed up over time. I recommend working with a metronome. Match the picking to the click.

By doing it this way, you will be able to improve your speed and articulation over time as you become more comfortable. Remember, playing the guitar is about an intimate connection that you make with the instrument through hours of practice.

Tremolo picking:

This is the same thing, except you do it faster, double-time. This is where the speed truly kicks in. But you must master alternate picking first before you can move to tremolo picking.

Example #1: On the low E string

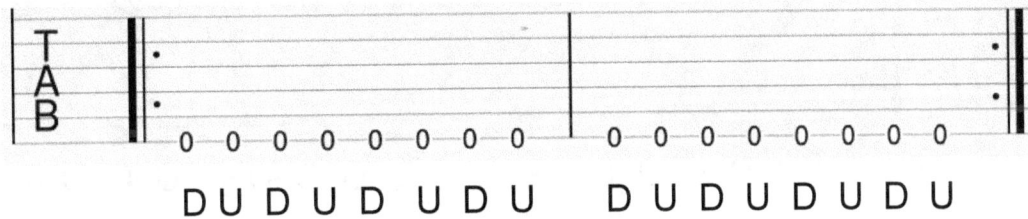

D U D U D U D U   D U D U D U D U

Example #2: With the Open E chord

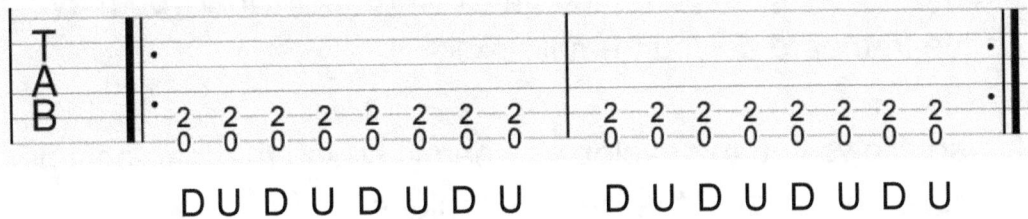

D U D U D U D U   D U D U D U D U

In these two above examples, you do the same thing you did with alternate picking, except you use tremolo picking. Double-time your wrist action.

Doing this on the 6th string (Low E) allows you to develop rhythm playing. Start with the 6th string open, then progress to playing the open E chord.

Exercise #3: On the high E string

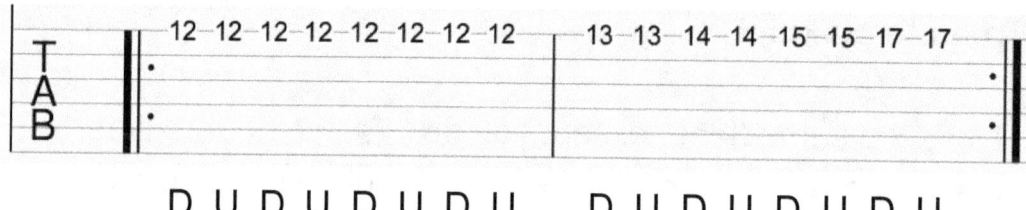

D U D U D U D U   D U D U D U D U

Exercise #4: Going higher up the fretboard

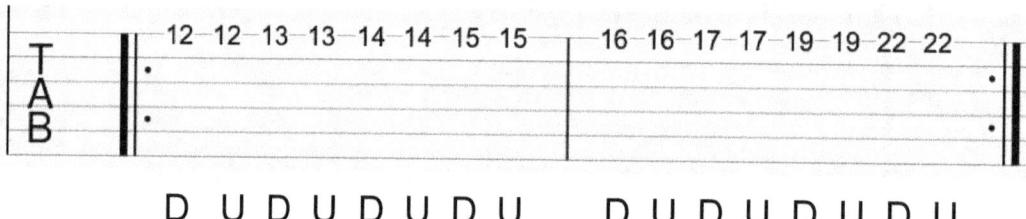

D U D U D U D U   D U D U D U D U

As you can see, these are very similar to the ones in the alternate picking lesson. The only difference is that you move up the fretboard as you tremolo pick.

It also allows you to develop a dynamic sound that can only be produced by utilizing this great technique.

Your guitar pick:
Make sure that you use just the tip of the pick when doing alternate or tremolo picking. It will help to reduce the friction caused by hitting the string so rapidly. Especially when hitting multiple strings while playing chords along the 6th string.

Alternate and tremolo picking are the two techniques you need to master to play shred guitar. Period! Everything else matters as well, but if you want to shred, you must master these two techniques.

Benefits of Alternate Picking:

1. Increased speed
2. Improved precision
3. Economy of motion

Benefits of Tremolo picking:

1. Expressive sound
2. Versatility
3. Improved dexterity

By incorporating these two wonderful techniques into your playing, you can not only enhance your expression of the notes along the fretboard but also expand your song repertoire.

Both techniques offer unique benefits and can be mastered with practice, patience, and perseverance. If you acquire this, you will soon be making sounds with your guitar that truly turn heads.

But you must be committed to the cause!

Chapter V Summary

First, we learned about how to bring the scales to life through personality traits. These techniques give the notes within the scales a personality. We will first start with hammer-ons and pull-offs.

Second, we then learn about slides and string bends. These are where you will either slide up and down from one note to another, or you will manipulate the note by bending it. Very common in lead guitar playing.

Third, we learn about trills and vibrato. Two very common techniques. Trills are repeated hammer-ons, and vibrato is where you vibrate the string after you pick it. Very much like a singer who vibrates a note with their vocal cords.

Fourth, we learn about triplets and melodic shapes. These are where you create music wth just a few notes. Triplets would be three notes repeated, and melodic shapes would be note patterns you ascend and descend along the fretboard.

Lastly, we learn about alternate and tremolo picking. Two techniques that are essential to lead guitar shredding. You must get these two techniques down, or there will be no shred for you. Practice, practice, practice.

Chapter VI: Phrasing With Guitar Licks

Lesson 26: What are guitar licks?

Guitar licks are short sequences of notes that are often used in riffs, solos, and melody lines. They are the building blocks of many famous songs and are well worth taking the time to learn about.

They are essential in many styles of music, such as Rock, Jazz, Blues & Country. Guitar licks can range from simple to more complex. Depending on what the application is that they are used for.

There are many benefits to learning guitar licks:

1. Improves Your Technical Skills
Practicing guitar licks helps you to develop and refine your technical abilities, such as finger dexterity, picking accuracy, and timing. As you tackle different licks, you'll encounter techniques like the ones learned within this book.

2. Enhances Musical Vocabulary
By learning to play a diverse range of guitar licks, you expand your musical vocabulary and enhance your creativity. This

allows you to express a wider array of emotions within your playing. As your skill set grows, you find it easier to create guitar solos and melody lines of your own.

3. Boosts Improvisational Skills

Guitar licks serve as an excellent foundation for improvisation. By memorizing and internalizing these phrases, you can spontaneously incorporate them into your solos. This will allow you to connect more deeply with your audience.

4. Strengthens Ear Training

When you learn guitar licks by ear, you hone your listening skills. This practice trains your ear to recognize pitch, rhythm, and dynamics. This can help with learning new songs more quickly and giving you ideas for compositions of your own.

5. Inspires Creativity

Learning guitar licks from different artists not only gives you insight into how they approach the instrument, but can also spark inspiration and creativity. By adding your own flair, you can develop a style that sets you apart from others.

There are many more benefits, but these five will get you started. Make sure to think about them as you study and learn guitar licks. You will soon realize how beneficial they can be to your guitar playing.

Lesson 27: Guitar licks within pattern one

Now that we have learned some common personality traits like hammer-ons and pull-offs, we can put them together to create guitar licks. This is what will help us to develop lead guitar phrasing.

We have also learned the five pentatonic scales, so we will learn guitar licks within these to see how they are used in context. This lesson will work with guitar licks within pattern one of the minor pentatonic.

Since rock and blues are more minor than major, we will learn from a minor point of view, but remember, you can always use the majors as well. Why? Because they are the same, just applied from a different point of view.

The more you understand how to apply the five pentatonic scales in both major and minor situations, the better you will be able to master the guitar fretboard and enhance your overall musicianship.

Guitar lick example #1: Use of the bend

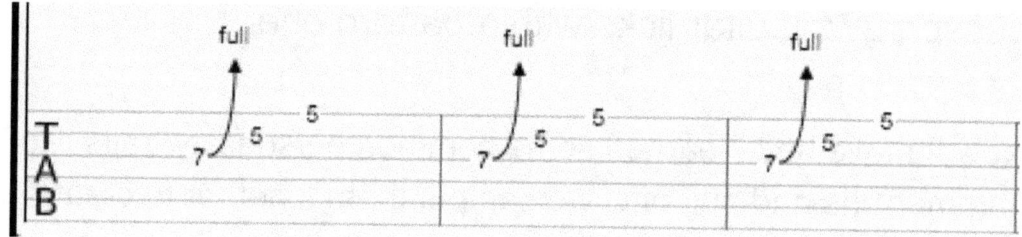

In this first example, we pick and bend the 5th note on the third string, then pick the 5th fret on the 2nd string, and the 5th fret on the first string. A three-note sequence.

Guitar lick example #2: Use of the pull-off

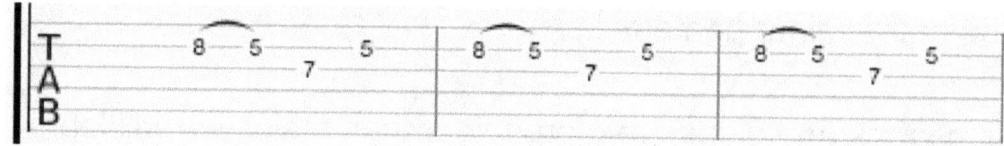

In this example, we pick the 8th fret on the 2nd string, pull-off to the 5th fret, and proceed to the 7th fret on the 3rd string, and back to the 5th fret on the 2nd string.

As you can see, these licks come out of pattern one of the minor pentatonic scale. The rest of the licks you learn from this lesson will as well.

This helps you to not only master guitar licks, but also master the minor pentatonic scale.

Guitar lick example #3:

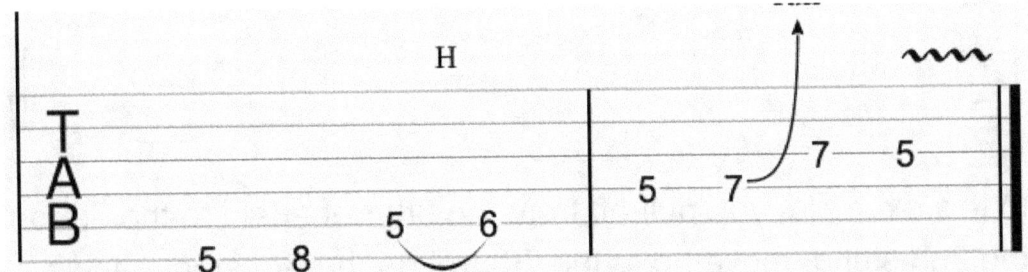

In this example, you pick the 5th and 8th notes on the 6th string, then hammer-on from the 5th to the 8th on the 5th string, and proceed to the fourth string at the 5th fret.

You then bend the 7th fret on the fourth string and move down to the 3rd string for the last two notes at the 7th and 5th frets. Using vibrato to end the lick.

Guitar lick example #4:

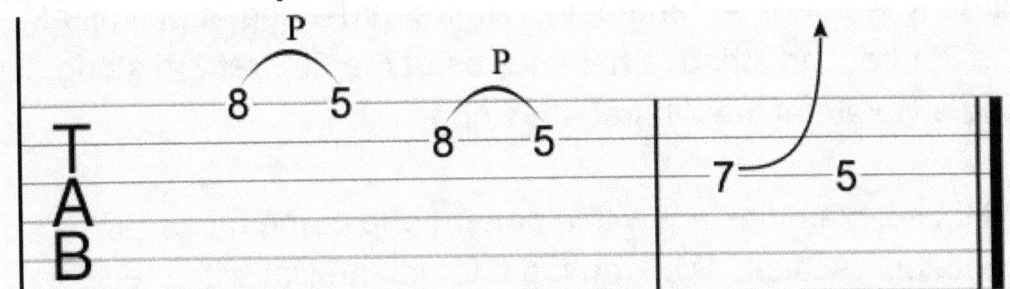

In this example, you pull-off from the 8th fret to the 5th on both the 1st and 2nd strings, then move to the 3rd string, pick and bend the 7th fret, and finish the lick on the 5th fret on the 3rd string.

Guitar lick example #5:

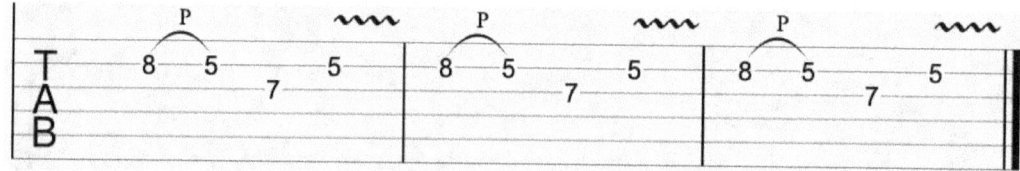

In this example, you pull-off from the 8th fret again to the 5th on the 2nd string, move up to the 7th fret on the 3rd string, and then back down to the 5th fret on the 2nd string. Once again, you finish off the lick with vibrato.

Guitar lick example #6:

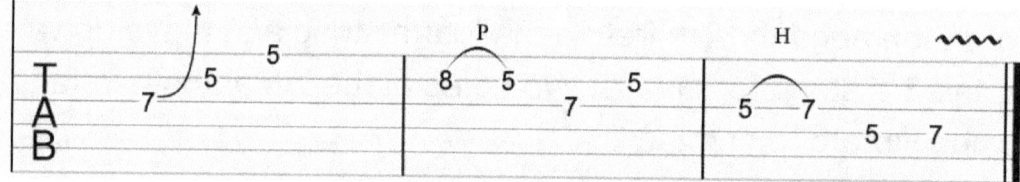

In this example, you mix and match some of what you have already learned. A bend at the 7th fret 3rd string, a pull-off at the 8th fret 2nd string, a hammer-on at the 5th fret 3rd string, and a vibrato at the 7th fret 4th string.

All these examples are within pattern one of the minor pentatonic scales. Work on them to get familiar with the scale pattern and guitar licks you can create within it.

Lesson 28: Guitar licks in patterns two & three

Now we will take a look at guitar licks in minor patterns two and three. Since the five patterns are all different, they offer a versatile and expressive foundation for creating guitar licks.

Example #1 Pattern 2: Pull-offs, bend, and vibrato

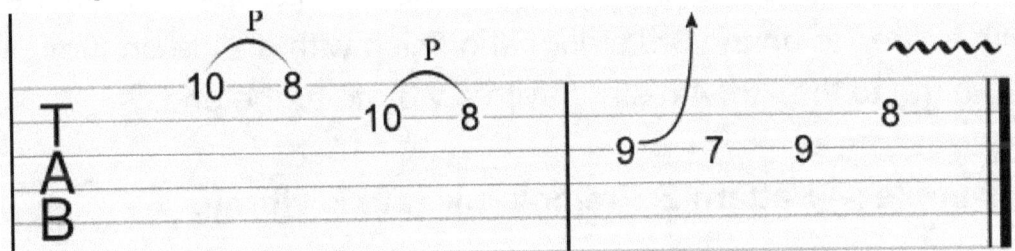

In this example, we use pull-offs at the 10th fret on the 1st and 2nd strings, then proceed with a bend on the 9th fret 3rd string, and finish with a vibrato on the 8th fre 2nd string.

Example #2 Pattern 2: Slides and vibrato

In this example, we use the slide on the 7th fret 4th string, 7th fret 3rd string, 8th fret 2nd string, and end with vibrato on the 8th fret of the 1st string.

Example #3 Pattern 2: Tremolo picking, pull-off & vibrato

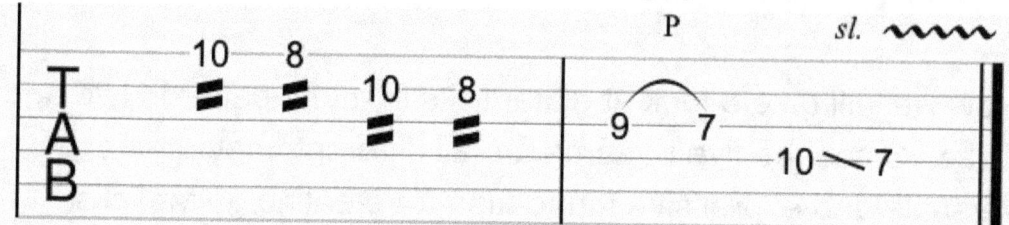

In this example, we use tremolo picking at the 10th and 8th frets on the 1st and 2nd strings, then proceed with a pull-off from the 9th to the 7th on the 3rd string, and finish with a slide on the 10th fret to the 7th, 4th string with a vibrato at the end.

Example #4 Pattern 2: Tremolo picking & vibrato

In this example, we use tremolo picking on the 7th, 9th, 8th, and 10th frets, and end the lick with vibrato on the 10th fret, 2nd string.

Practice these guitar licks within pattern two until you can play them easily. You'll see very clearly how they will begin to enhance your guitar playing. Especially the tremolo picking. Like I said before, if you want to shred, you've got to get this technique down!

Guitar licks within pattern three

Example #1 Pattern 3: Hammer-ons, slide & vibrato

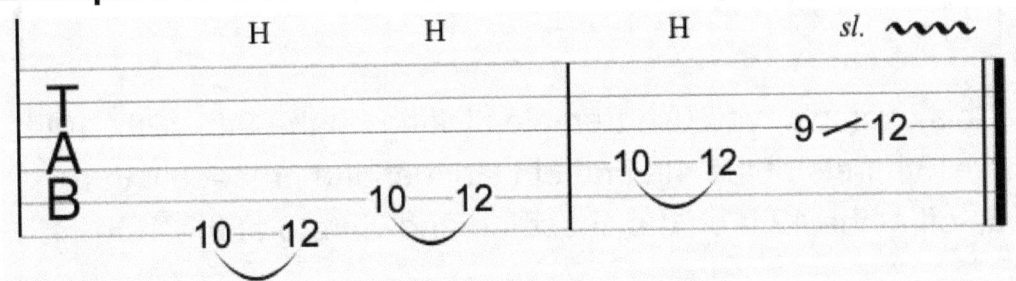

In this example, you hammer-on from the 10th fret to the 12th on the 6th, 5th, and 4th strings, slide from the 9th to the 12th fret on the 3rd string, and end the lick with a vibrato on the 12th.

Example #2 Pattern 3: Hammer-ons, slides & vibrato

In this example, you use two pull-offs at the 12th and 13th frets, proceed to slides at the 12th to 9th frets, and end the lick with a vibrato on the 10th fret.

Example #3 Pattern 3: Tremolo picking, pull-off & vibrato

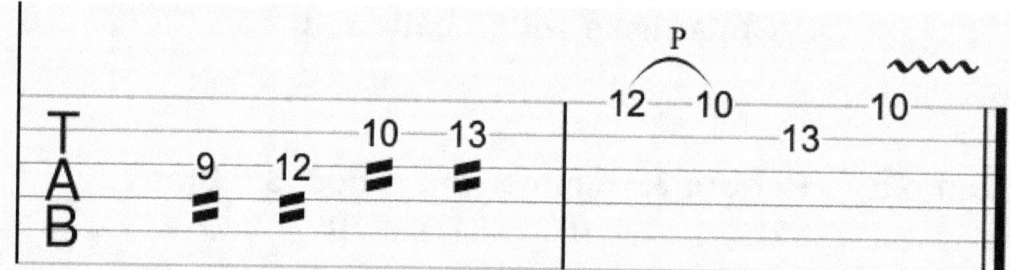

In this example, you use tremolo picking on the 9th, 12th, 10th, and 13th frets of the 4th and 5th strings, and proceed wth a pull-off at the 12th on the 1st string and vibrato at the 10th.

Example #4 Pattern 3: bend, vibrato, and a pull-off

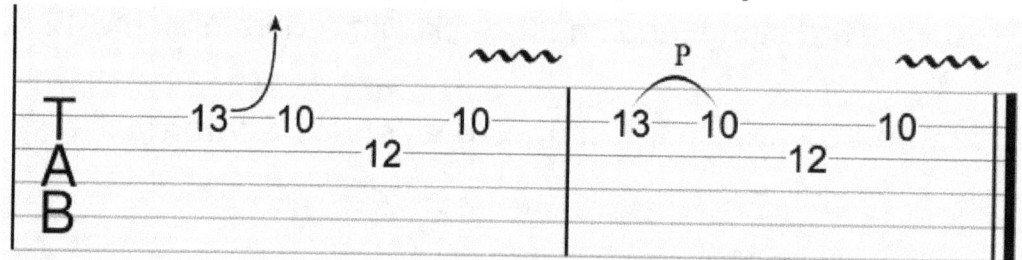

In this example, you start with a bend on the 13th fret of the 2nd string, add a vibrato on the 10th fret of the 2nd string, and pull-off the 13th fret to the 10th on the 2nd string, and end the lick with a vibrato on the 10th fret of the 2nd string.

*Study and practice these daily.

Lesson 29: Guitar licks in patterns four & five

Now we come to the next two patterns, patterns four and five. These are also different from the other three and can provide for some exciting guitar licks.

Example #1 Pattern 4: Pull-off and vibrato

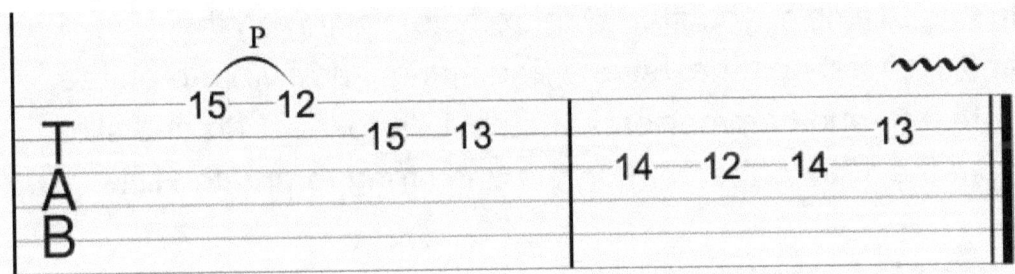

In this example, you pull-off from the 15th fret to the 12th on the 1st string, proceed through the pattern, and end the lick with a vibrato on the 13th fret of the 2nd string.

Example #2 Pattern 4: Bend, pull-off, & vibrato

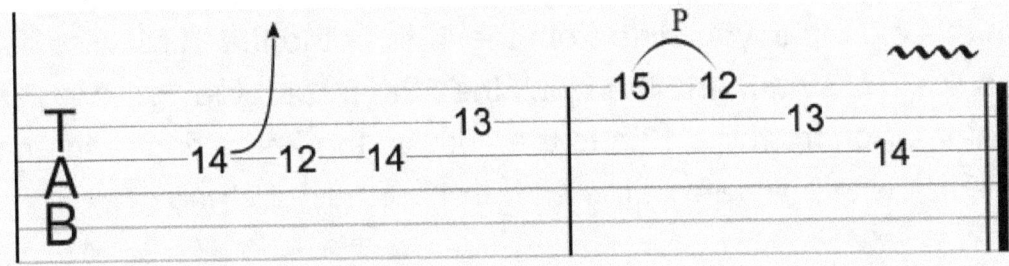

In this example, you pick and bend the 14th fret 3rd string, proceed through the pattern, pull-off on the 15th fret to the 12th on the 1st string, and end the lick with a vibrato on the 14th fret.

Example #3 Pattern 4:

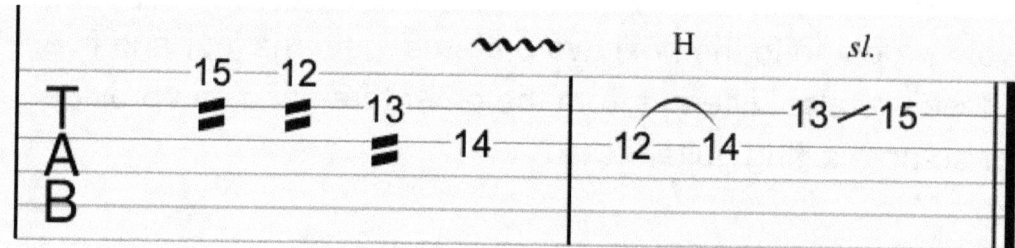

In this example, you start with tremolo picking on the 15th, 12th, and 13th frets on the 1st and 2nd strings, add vibrato on the 14th fret, and hammer-on from the 12th to the 14th and slide from the 13th to the 15th on the 2nd string to end the lick.

Example #4 Pattern 4:

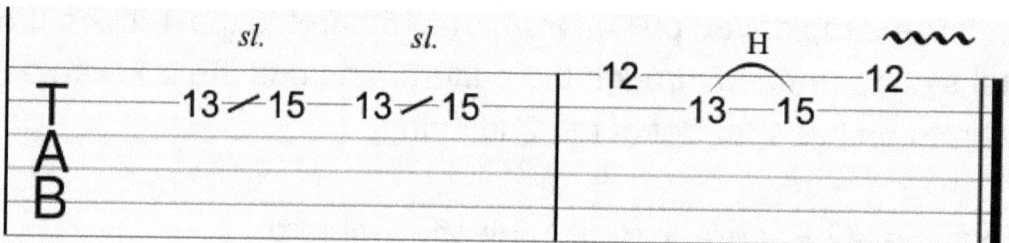

In this example, you slide from the 13th fret to the 15th twice, on the 2nd string, and then pick the 12th fret on the 1st string, hammer-on from the 13th to the 15th on the 2nd string, and end the lick with a vibrato at the 12th fret on the 1st string.

*Although you're learning these at this part of the fretboard, they can be played anywhere.

Now, let's take a look at a few guitar licks within pattern five. Since this pattern is different, you will have more opportunities for guitar lick creativity.

Example #1 Pattern 5: Pull-offs & vibrato

In this example, you use pull-offs and vibrato at the 17th & 15th frets. Watch for the string change in this lick from strings 1 and 2 to 3 and 4.

Example #2 Pattern 5: Tremolo picking & vibrato

In this example, you use tremolo picking starting at the 17th fret on the 1st string and proceed through the pattern. You then end the lick with vibrato at the 15th fret, 1st string.

*Remember, when doing tremolo picking, use the tip of the pick for less friction, and keep the picking hand close to the strings for minimal wrist movement.

Example #3 Pattern 5: Tremolo picking & vibrato

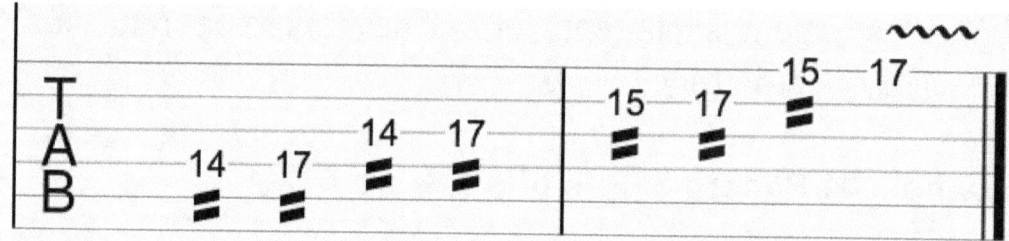

In this example, you also use tremolo picking, but starting at the 14th fret on the 4th string. You continue with this technique on the 3rd and 2nd strings until you end at the 17th fret of the 1st string with vibrato.

Example #4 Pattern 5: Slides, pull-off & vibrato

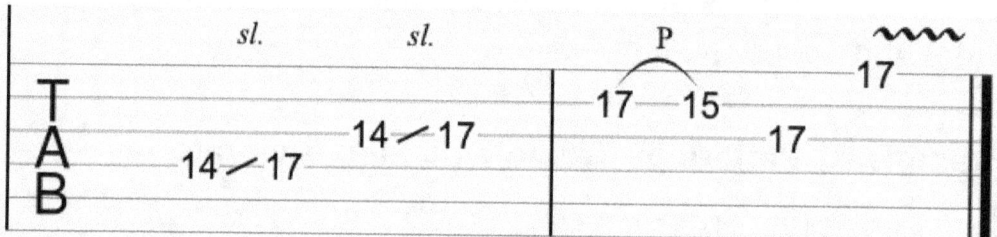

In this example, you use slides starting at the 14th fret on the 4th string. You repeat this on the 3rd string, do a pull-off at the 17th fret on the 2nd string, and end the lick with a vibrato on the 17th of the 1st string.

What's cool about this pattern in the key of A minor is that you can also play it at the 3rd fret. So instead of you playing at the 15th to 17th frets, you'd play from the 3rd to the 5th.

Same pattern, just different location. Try these here too.

Lesson 30: Guitar licks in multiple patterns & tips

Now that you know how to play guitar licks within each of the 5 pentatonic patterns, we will now look at how to play guitar licks using multiple patterns. This will help you to master more of the fretboard.

Example #1 Patterns 1 & 2: Slides & vibrato

In this example, you start at the 5th fret 6th string, use a slide at the 5th fret 5th string, and at the 7th fret 3rd string, and end with vibrato on the 9th fret 3rd string.

Example #2 Patterns 2 & 3: Pull-off, hammer-on & slides

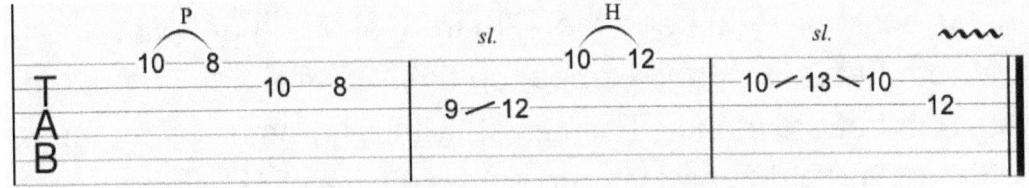

In this example, you start with a pull-off at the 10th fret 1st string, use a slide on the 9th fret 3rd string, a hammer-on on the 10th fret 1st string, as well as slides on the 10th fret 2nd string, and finish with a vibrato on the 12th fret 3rd string.

Try to visualize the patterns as you play through them.

Example #3 Patterns 3 & 4: Tremolo, hammer-on & pull-off

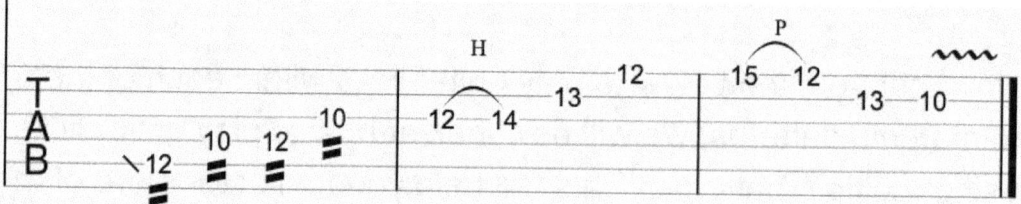

In this example, you slide up to the 12th fret 5th string, and tremolo pick to the 10th fret 3rd string. Then proceed with a hammer-on on the 12th fret 3rd string, pull-off on the 15th fret 1st string, and end with vibrato on the 10th fret 2nd string.

Example #4 Patterns 4 & 5: Bends & vibrato

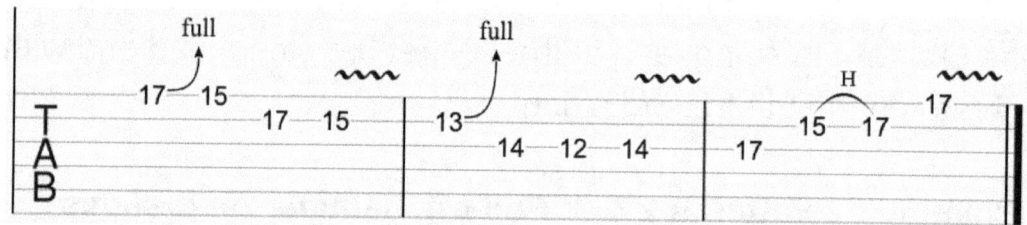

In this example, you bend the 17th fret 1st string and vibrato on the 15th fret 2nd string. Repeat on the 13th fret 2nd string and the 14th fret 3rd string. Then finish with a hammer-on on the 15th fret 2nd string and vibrato on the 17th fret 1st string.

Don't be afraid to mix and match ideas. As long as you stay within the patterns, you can't go wrong.

*Remember, once you master the road map, you can drive with confidence anywhere along the fretboard.

Tips For Mastering Guitar Licks

- **Practice Slowly:** Start each lick at a slow tempo to ensure accuracy before gradually increasing speed. This will help with improving finger dexterity.

- **Use a Metronome:** A metronome will help you maintain consistent timing as you progress. This is a very important skill to develop.

- **Experiment with Dynamics:** Varying your pick attack and volume can add expressiveness to your licks. This will help develop new techniques.

- **Incorporate Vibrato:** Adding vibrato can enhance the emotional impact of your playing. A hard technique to master, so work on it daily.

By exploring these patterns and licks daily as part of your practice routine, you will expand your fretboard knowledge as well as improve your improvisational skills.

But you must be diligent. Shred guitar does not come overnight and requires the most serious commitment.

Chapter VI Summary

First, we learn about guitar licks. What they are and how they can be utilized to create phrasing. These are short sequences of notes that are used to create guitar riffs, solos, and melody lines.

Second, we learn guitar licks within the minor pentatonic scale pattern one. Since rock and blues are more minor than major, we will look at them within these scale patterns. Starting with pattern one.

Third, we then learn guitar licks within patterns two and three. Since the scale patterns are different, they offer a variety of options to pull from. Pattern two offers guitar licks that are different from patterns one and three.

Fourth, we then learn guitar licks within patterns four and five. Since these are different from the other three, they can add some exciting options for phasing. Notice how pattern five in A minor can be played in two positions.

Lastly, we look at guitar licks within multiple scale patterns that allow us to extend our phrasing options along the fretboard. As well as tips for mastering guitar licks. Remember, guitar licks are the essence of phrasing.

Chapter VII: Major Scale Modes

Lesson 31: The Ionian & Dorian modes

Another type of scale patterns that are very common for shredding guitar is the modes. These are 7 patterns that come out of the major scale. Seven notes equal seven modes.

Each mode is based on the 7 notes in the scale. In the key of C major, the notes would be: C-D-E-F-G-A-B. The Ionian would be based on the first note, C, and the Dorian would be based on the second note, D, etc.

1. **C = Ionian**
2. **D = Dorian**
3. **E = Phrygian**
4. **F = Lydian**
5. **G = Mixolydian**
6. **A = Aeolian**
7. **B = Locrian**

I know these have strange names, but don't let that deter you from using them. They can be very helpful in not only shredding the guitar, but also in unlocking the mysteries of the fretboard. In both lead and rhythm playing.

In this lesson, we will look at the first two. The Ionian mode and the Dorian mode. Remember, these can be looked at as patterns. Just like the pentatonics, the difference with these, though, is that there are 7 instead of 5, and they use more notes per string.

This allows for even more creative musical ideas. Let's look at the first mode, the Ionian, which is essentially the major scale. For easier learning, we will learn these in the key of G major.

The G Ionian mode: 1 2 3 4 5 6 7

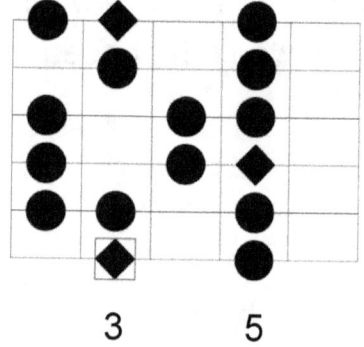

3   5

This mode will start on the G note, which is the 3rd fret on the 6th string. The diamond shapes indicate the root note (G) that resides within the scale.

In the scale of G major, the formula will be:

G A B C D E & F#. These 7 notes are where the 7 modes will be based in this key. G Ionian, A Dorian, B Phrygian, etc, etc.

The second mode we will look at is the Dorian. This mode always resides on the 2nd tone degree.

The A Dorian mode: A B C D E F# G

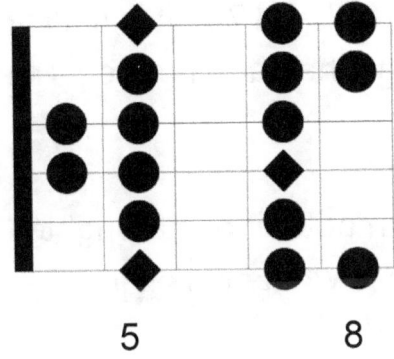

5   8

In the key of G major, this mode will start on the 5th fret on the 6th string because that is where the A note is. You can also play it at the 17th fret because that is an A note as well.

In this mode, we will be flattening the 3rd and 7th notes. It is what will give this mode its character. The Dorian will have the same notes, just start on the A instead of the G.

Ionian mode: 1 2 3 4 5 6 7
Dorian mode: 1 2 b3 4 5 6 b7

Can you see how this affects the sound? With the 3rd being flattened, this also lets us know that this mode is minor, and since it has the flat 7th, it will fit great over minor 7th chords.

The reason for this is that the minor 7th chord has a flat 3rd and 7th notes in it. Modes work great with chord theory as well, so they can be very beneficial to learn along your guitar playing journey.

Since the Dorian mode has only the flat 3rd and 7th, it is similar to the natural minor scale, which also has the flat 6th note. This gives it a different shade of color.

Since the Dorian mode has the major 6th note, it has a brighter sound than the natural minor. This note is what gives it its unique tone quality.

Natural minor: 1 2 b3 4 5 b6 b7
Dorian minor: 1 2 b3 4 5 6 b7

Can you see the difference? When playing the Dorian mode, you want to expose this character difference. By adding the Dorian mode to your improvising, you add a new dimension to your music, as well as enhance your playing skills.

Go through the two modes in this chapter like you did the pentatonics. Create guitar licks within them. By doing this, you will develop different types of riffs, solos, and melody lines.

This will allow you to express different emotions in your music as well as master more of the fretboard.

Lesson 32: The Phrygian & Lydian modes

Now that we have identified the first two modes, we can look at the next two. The Phrygian mode and the Lydian mode. These will reside on the next two note intervals of the scale, and since we're using the scale of G major, they will be on B & C.

Let's look at this in more detail:

B Phrygian mode: B C D E F# G A
C Lydian mode: C D E F# G A B

As you can see, they use the same notes. It's just what note you start on that makes the difference.

B Phrygian mode: B C D E F# G A

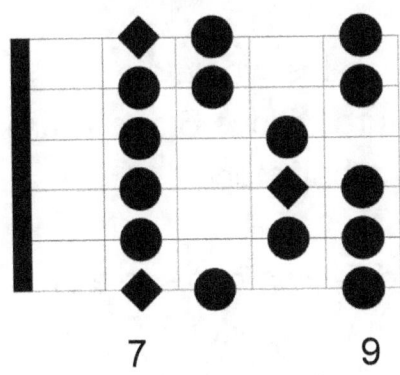

7   9

The B Phrygian mode will start at the 7th fret on the 6th string because that is where this note is located. The 3rd degree of G major. Basically, a B minor scale with the flat 2 added.

In theory, music is a science of mathematics. This is because you use numbers and formulas. A whole step is 2 frets, and a half step is one fret. With this information, we can see the scientific formula for each mode.

This is what you want to master within each mode. Because it is these whole steps and half steps that give each mode its individual character.

If you look at the modes we have learned so far, you will see these formulas in them. Let's use the Phrygian mode as an example.

Phrygian mode: B C D E F# G A
1 b2 b3 4 5 b6 b7
H W W W H W

From a scientific point of view, we can see the whale step, half-step formula within the mode structure. Since B and C are next to each other, we can see that it is a half step,

Since there are two frets between E and F#, we can see this is a whole step. These 7 notes consist of 4 whole steps and 2 half steps. If you look at the other modes you learned so far, these will be different. This goes for all 7 modes.

*This is what gives each mode its character.

Now, let's look at the 4th mode in the G major scale, the Lydian mode. Just like the Phrygian mode, this will start on the next tone degree of the major scale. In this case, it will be the C note.

The C note resides at the 8th fret on the 6th string, and this is where the Lydian mode will start in the key of G major.

C Lydian mode: C D E F# G A B

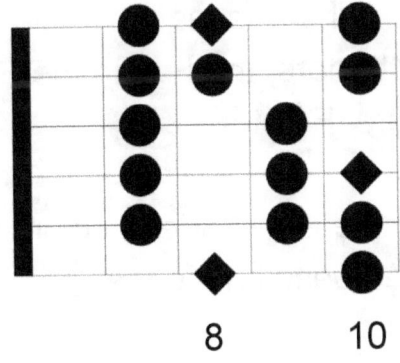

8   10

If you look closely at this scale, you will see that it is exactly like the Phrygian, except it starts on the C note. What this does is it changes the character dramatically. When a scale or chord has a flat 3rd note in it, it is considered minor.

A natural 3rd note is considered major, and if you look closely at these two modes that reside next to each other, one has the characteristics of a minor, and the other a major. Why? Because of the note formula.

B Phrygian mode: 1 b2 b3 4 5 b6 b7

Since this mode has the flat 3rd in it, we know it is minor, and will reflect this dark sound when we play it. On the other hand, the Lydian mode has a natural 3rd note.

C Lydian mode: 1 2 3 #4 5 6 7

The E note is natural in the C Lydian mode, and this gives it a different tone aspect than the Phrygian. What makes the Lydian mode special is the sharpened 4th note, the F#. In the key of C major, this would just be a natural F note.

This F# note is what gives this mode a different shade of color from the Ionian mode. The Ionian mode doesn't have the raised (sharpened) 4th note.

A major scale gives an uplifting, happy type of sound, and when you sharpen the 4th note in it, like in the Lydian mode, it gives it a different shade of uplifting emotion.

Each mode has a different character, and it is your job to discover that character and bring it out in your playing.

The first four modes:

G Ionian mode: G A B C D E F#
Mode formula: 1 2 3 4 5 6 7

A Dorian mode: A B C D E F# G
Mode formula: 1 2 b3 4 5 6 b7

B Phrygian mode: B C D E F# G A
Mode formula: 1 b2 b3 4 5 b6 b7

C Lydian mode: C D E F# G A B
Mode formula: 1 2 3 #4 5 6 7

Notice how they all have the same 7 notes, but start on a different one. It is this note placement that gives them a different tonal quality. Which can be used for many different applications.

By the information above, you should be able to figure out the whole-step, half-step formula for each mode. I recommend you get a separate piece of paper and do so. This will help you to better understand them.

*Remember, the placement of the 3rd note will determine which are major and which are minor.

Lesson 33: The Mixolydian & Aeolian modes

We now come to the 5th and 6th modes in the scale, the Mixolydian and Aeolian modes. These will either be major or minor modes. How do we determine this? By the placement of the 3rd note.

We will first start with the Mixolydian mode. In this mode, it is natural. This suggests a major aspect, and also lets us know what type of sound we can expect from it.

D Mixolydian mode: D E F# G A B C

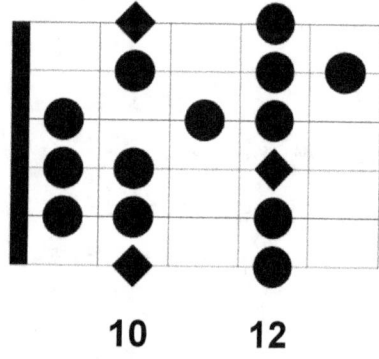

10   12

Once again, since we are in the key of G major and the Mixolydian mode is on the 5th tone degree, the D note, we will play this at the 10th fret.

This is a major mode, but the placement of the notes tells us that it is different from the other two major modes we learned.

What is the difference? Well, let's take a look.

D Mixolydian mode: D E F# G A B C
Mode formula: 1 2 3 4 5 6 b7

Ah, it has a flat 7th note in it. This is what makes it have a different shade of color than the other two major modes.

G Ionian mode: 1 2 3 4 5 6 7
C Lydian mode: 1 2 3 #4 5 6 7
D Mixolydian mode: 1 2 3 4 5 6 b7

Can you see how these three modes are all major, but slightly different in character? This is what makes them individually unique.

This is what you will discover as you go through them. Do this enough, and you will see how you can pull different guitar licks out of each one and how they all sound slightly different because of these note intervals.

This is important to remember when creating emotion with your guitar. Deciding what kind of emotion is conveyed in a song you learn, or possibly in a composition of your own.

Now let's look at the next mode in the sequence, the E Aeolian mode. This mode is the natural minor mode because it has the flat 3rd as well as the flat 6th and 7th notes in it.

E Aeolian mode: 1 2 b3 4 5 b6 b7

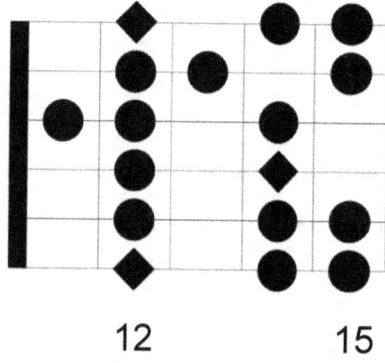

12   15

As you can see, this mode will start on the 12th fret of the 6th string because, like before with the other modes, this is where the E note is. Each mode will be located on its specific tone degree within the key you choose to play it in.

You just need to know the notes of the key, and you're set to find them every time.

This scale will have a somber, mournful sound to it and will be a great choice for that type of emotion within a composition.

*The natural minor will always be the 6th tone degree in any major scale. Knowing this will make it easier to find.

Now we have three minor modes.

A Dorian mode: A B C D E F# G
Mode formula: 1 2 b3 4 5 6 b7

B Phrygian mode: B C D E F# G A
Mode formula: 1 b2 b3 4 5 b6 b7

E Aeolian mode: E F# G A B C D
Mode formula: 1 2 b3 4 5 b6 b7

Just like the three major modes we looked at earlier, we can see that these are slightly different. All are made up of the same notes, but since their note formulas are different, they each have a different character.

So, when you're crafting out your next million seller hit, you can choose from a wide variety of emotions to convey. Whether they're uplifting, like with the major, or somber, like with the minor.

*Remember, the 1st, 4th, and 5th modes are always going to be major, and the 2nd, 3rd, and 6th modes are going to be minor. All residing within any major key.

So what does that make the 7th mode? Well, let's find out.

Lesson 34: The Locrian mode & basic modal theory

We now come to the 7th and final of the modes, the Locrian mode. This is a very interesting mode because it is different from the other six.

It's not major or minor, it's diminished.

Diminished?

Yes, diminished. The reason for this is that it has a flat 5th note in it, and if you look at the other six, none of them have that.

Interesting huh?

This makes this mode very unique and great for very dark, moody compositions, like in heavy metal music.

F# Locrian mode: F# G A B C D E

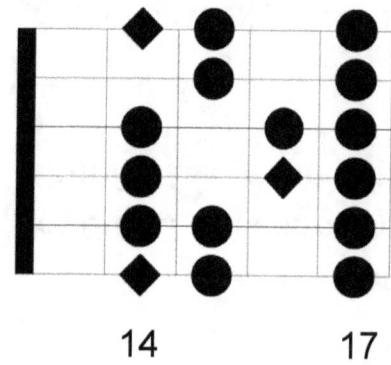

14   17

This mode incorporates elements of the other three minor modes. It has the flat 2nd, like the Phrygian, and the flat 6th and 7th, like the Dorian and Aeolian.

What makes it unique is the flat 5th. Whenever you have a flat 3rd and flat 5th note in a mode, scale, or chord, it is diminished.

Because it starts on the 7th tone degree of the major scale, it has a dissonant, unresolved sound to it that doesn't fit well with most styles of music.

But it can still be beneficial if used in the right context. Since it sounds the way it does, it can be effectively used in certain types of dark music to convey moody emotions.

A Dorian mode: 1 2 b3 4 5 6 b7

B Phrygian mode: 1 b2 b3 4 5 b6 b7

E Aeolian mode: 1 2 b3 4 5 b6 b7

F# Locrian mode: 1 b2 b3 4 b5 b6 b7

See how these all have the flat 3rd in common, but then they morph into their own character after that? This is what makes the modes so beneficial to know and use in your guitar playing.

Basic Scale Modal Theory

Understanding modes provides you with the ability to create more diverse and interesting sounds by altering and manipulating the notes.

Remember, modes are variations of a scale with each starting on a different tone degree within the scale. Like we have done in this chapter. Each has its own unique sequence of intervals, which gives it a distinct sound and character.

The seven modes are:

Ionian mode: Known as the major scale, it is the most familiar and widely used. Characterized by a bright, happy sound.

Dorian mode: This mode has a minor quality, but with a slightly brighter sound than the natural minor mode.

Phrygian mode: Known for its dark, exotic feel due to its distinctive half-step interval between the 1st two notes.

Lydian mode: This mode is similar to the major scale, but with a dreamy quality to it due to its raised fourth note.

Mixolydian mode: Known to have a dominant seventh sound quality because of the lowered 7th note.

Aeolian mode: Also known as the natural minor scale, it has a dark and moody sound quality.

Locrian mode: This mode has a diminished quality and is often considered unstable due to its flattened fifth interval.

Applying the modes

To apply the modes in your guitar playing, start by learning the major scale positions across the fretboard. Then practice playing each mode individually. This will help you to internalize their distinct sounds and integrate them into your playing.

Tips for practicing the modes:

- Focus on one mode at a time
- Play along with backing tracks
- Work on improvising

By understanding scale modal theory, you will be able to greatly expand your musical expression, allowing you to create richer, more varied compositions and solos.

If you'd like to dive deeper, I suggest you check out my other books, which I've authored specifically on the modes. These can be found where all books are sold.

Lesson 35: All seven modes in multiple keys

In this chapter, we will look at the modes in a few different keys. This will help you to identify them along the fretboard.

Key of A major: A B C# D E F# G#

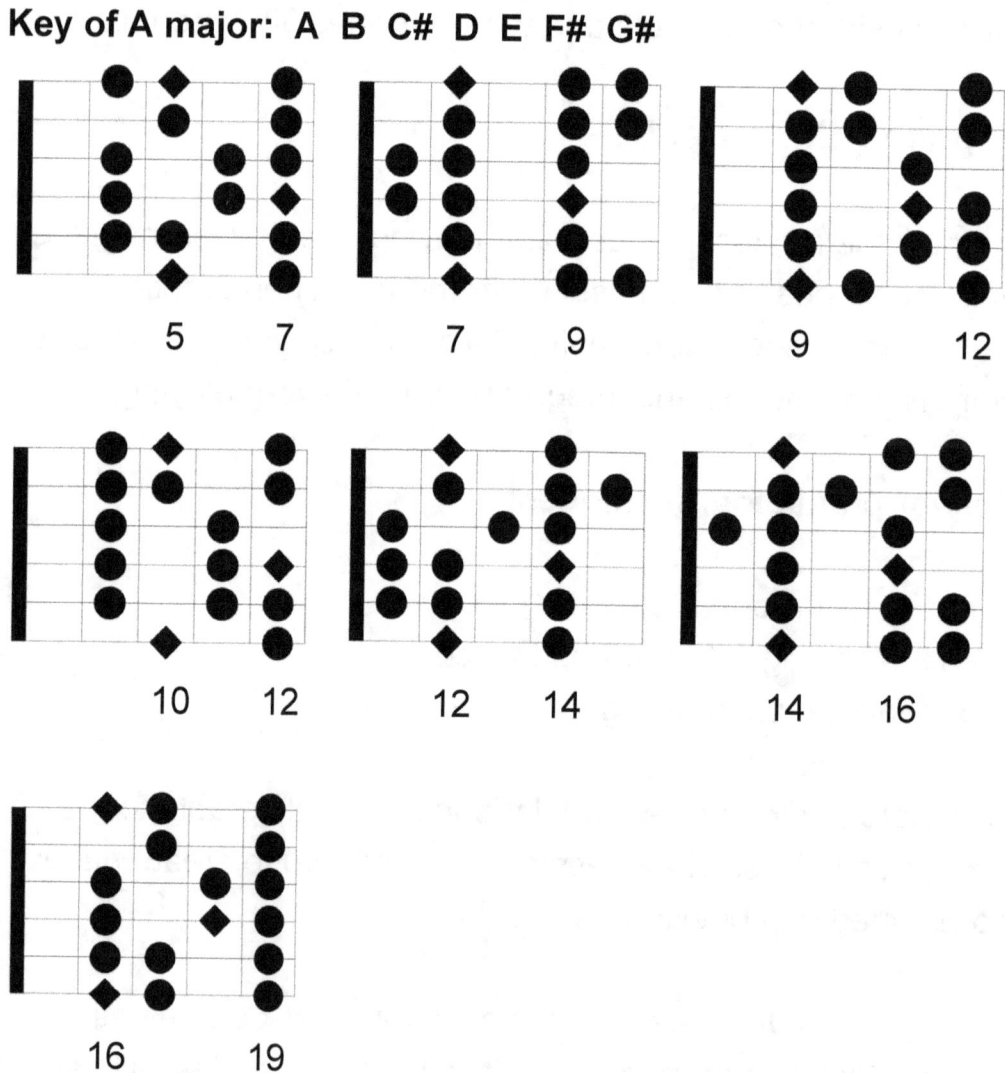

Key of C major: C D E F G A B

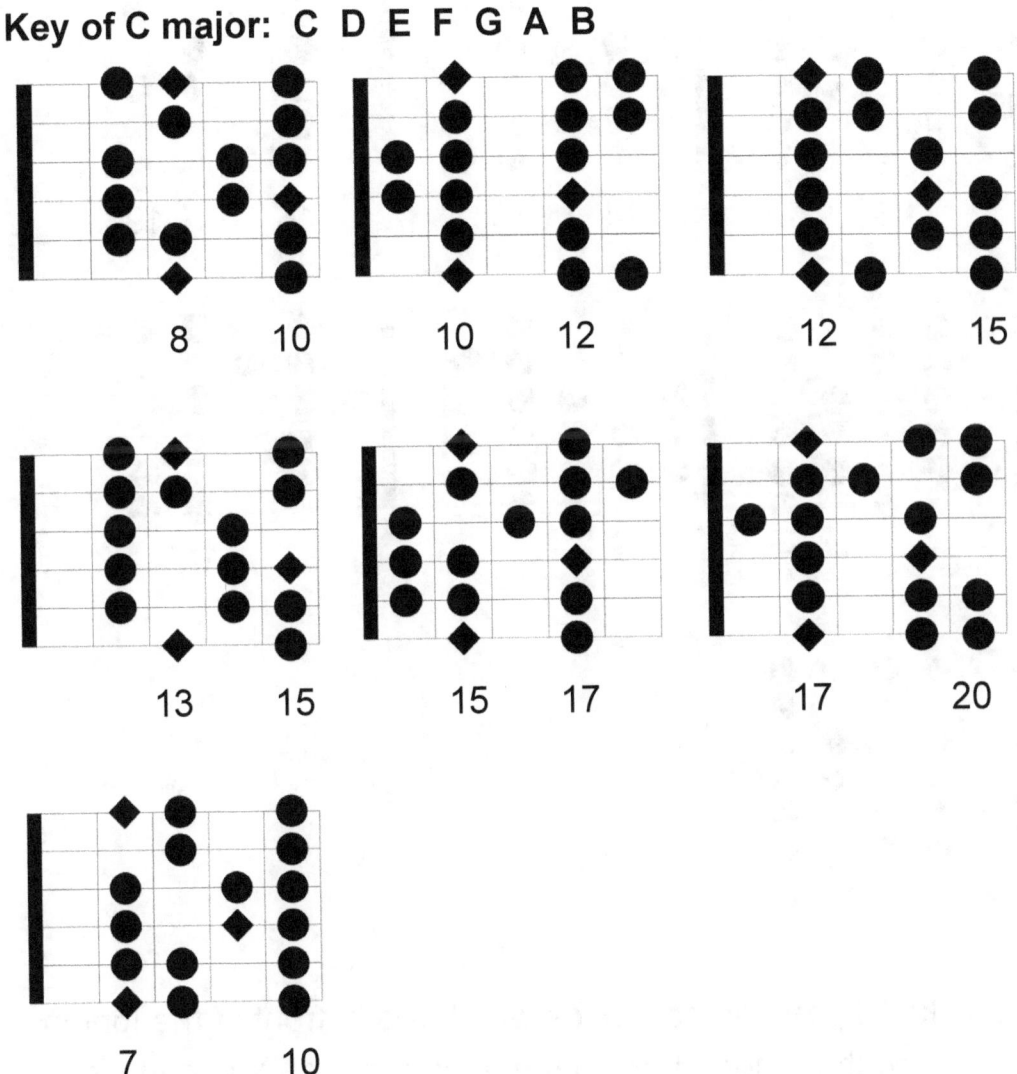

8   10   10   12   12   15

13   15   15   17   17   20

7   10

In the key of C major, I put the Locrian mode behind the Ionian mode because it will be easier to play in this position.
Especially if you only have 22 frets.

114

Key of E major: E F# G# A B C# D#

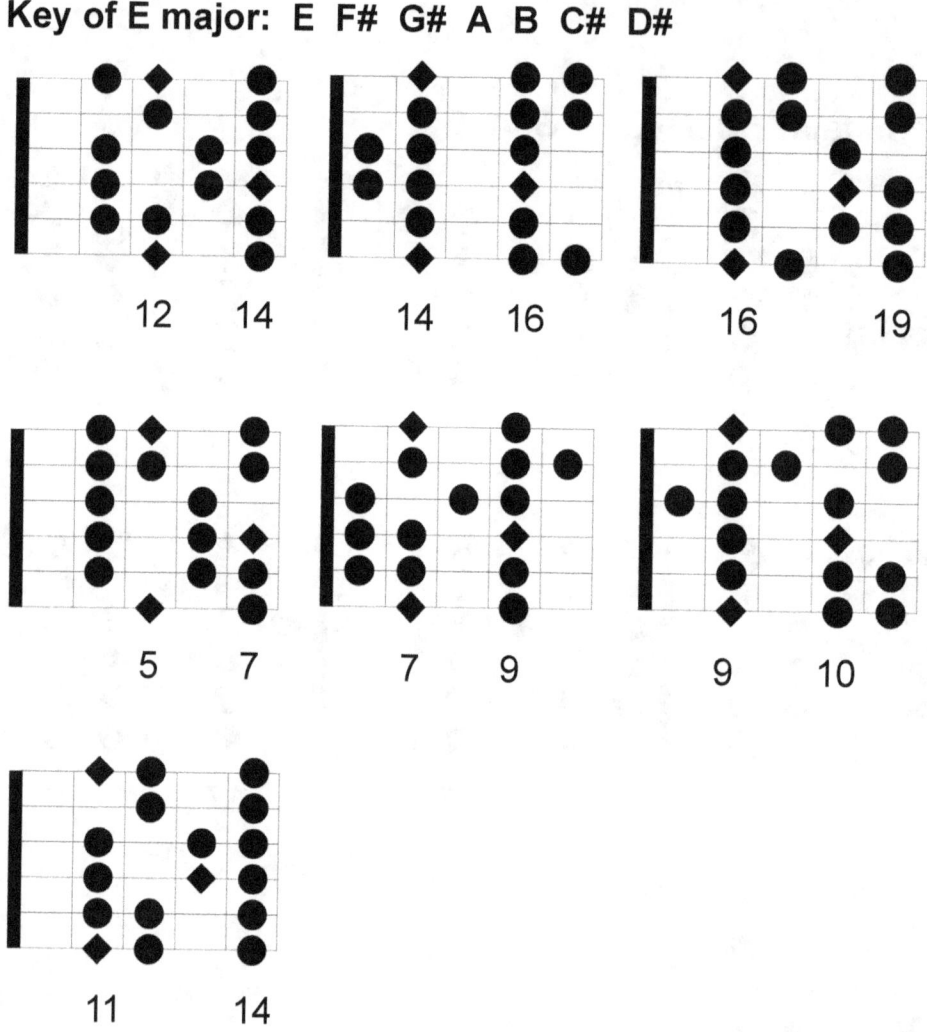

12　　14　　　　14　　16　　　　16　　　　19

5　　7　　　　7　　9　　　　9　　10

11　　　　14

In this key, I present the modes with three in front of the Ionian mode, and the other 4 behind the Ionian mode. You can also place the Dorian mode at the 2nd fret and the Phrygian mode at the 4th fret if you'd like.

This is a great key to work with because it is very common.

Remember, these span along the fretboard from root to octave (A to A, C to C, etc), and repeat just like the pentatonic scales. So, the objective is to get familiar with their shapes. Almost like puzzle pieces that connect.

Also, notice how the modes keep their individual shape even when presented in different keys. The Dorian shape will always be the same, no matter what key it is played in. It's just where it's located along the fretboard that will matter.

That's the great thing about the guitar: if you think in patterns, the notes will change and line up automatically without you having to think about it. That way, you can concentrate on playing and creating music.

Notice how in the three keys presented, the notes in the modes line up as they should. If you go through the Ionian mode in the key of A major, you will see that they conform to that key, and if you move it up to the 8th fret in C major, they do there, too.

Isn't that cool?

There is much that can be learned about the modes and how they can improve not only your playing, but also your overall musicianship and mastery of the fretboard. You just need to study and practice them daily.

Chapter VII Summary

First, we learned about the seven major scale modes. Also popular for playing shred guitar. We look at the first two, the Ionian and the Dorian modes. These are presented in the key of G major for easy learning.

Second, we learn the Phrygian and Lydian modes. These are the third and fourth modes within the major scale. In the key of G major, they will reside on the B and C notes. This will allow for more creativity within the scale.

Third, we learn about the Mixolydian and Aeolian modes. These will be the 5th and 6th modes, and will reside at the D and E notes. Notice how even though the scale notes stay the same, the mode formulas change.

Fourth, we learn about the last mode, the Locrian mode, and basic modal theory. What is neat about the Locrian mode is that it has the flat 5th note, which makes it diminished, and different from the other six.

Lastly, we look at all seven modes in multiple keys. The key of A major, C major, and E major. These are common keys that many songs are written in. Try these out in other keys to get familiar with them.

Chapter VIII: Additional Training

Lesson 36: Learning from recordings

In this chapter, we will examine some additional training that will help you to improve your guitar playing even more. In this particular lesson, we will look at learning from recordings.

Learning to play songs from recordings is a very valuable skill. It not only enhances your listening ability but also improves your understanding of how songs are constructed. This can be very beneficial when creating your own.

Here, we will look at tips and techniques to make your learning experience more effective.

Step 1: Choose The Right Song

Begin by picking a song that suits your current skill level. This is very important, as a song that is way above it will frustrate you when trying to learn it. As you become more familiar with the process, you can progress to harder songs.

Remember, this is a process, and it must be taken one step at a time for you to truly master it.

Step 2: Listen Actively

Actively listening is crucial when learning from recordings. It allows your ear to get familiar with the song structure and the techniques needed to play the song. The chord progression, the melody line, rhythm, etc.

Step 3: Break It Down

Breaking the song down into manageable sections can be a huge help in the learning process. Focus on one part at a time, like the verse or chorus. Then try linking the two parts together. This will make it less overwhelming.

Step 4: Find The Key To The Song

Work at finding the root note. A note or chord that is used a lot is usually the key of the song. Then start researching what chords are played in that key. This will help identify the chord progression.

Step 5: Persistence and Patience

Learning to play the guitar in this manner is not easy. It takes persistence and patience. This can only be done through daily practice. Do so, and you will master the art of learning from recordings and improving your listening skills.

Lesson 37: Improvising within a song

There are two things that you truly want to master when it comes to playing shred guitar.

1. **Playing solos as they are written**
2. **Improvising your own solos**

The reason why these two things are so important is that they develop two different skill sets. Playing solos as they are written develops discipline, and improvising your own develops creativity. Both are very important in playing the guitar.

In this chapter, we are going to look at the latter. Improvising within a song. This is a skill that most guitarists have an issue with. The reason for this is that there is no blueprint to follow.

Playing solos as they are written is hard too, but you at least have something to follow, but with improvising, you are going into no-man's land, so to speak. Which can be both exciting and scary at the same time.

So, we will look at some tips that can help you develop in this area. All the lessons you've learned up to this point will help tremendously in this area. So I recommend you make sure you study and practice them to get the most out of this skill set.

When improvising, it's good to understand the song structure, key, and chord progression if possible. Especially the key, as this will help you to know what notes to choose, and where to play your scales.

This is where your study and practice will pay off as you begin to identify these concepts. In a live performance situation, you will need to identify these things quickly.

#1 Identify the Key: Knowing the key of the song is crucial. It acts as a roadmap for your improvisation. It will give you the parameters of where to play and where not to. Kind of like coloring within the lines.

#2 Identify the Chords: If you have time, try to identify the chords within the song. This will help you know what notes will work when improvising.

#3 Choose your Scales: This is the fun part: choose your scales. The key will tell you where to play them, and keep you on the roadmap of the song.

#4 Practice, Practice, Practice: Being able to improvise with confidence takes time, study, and plenty of practice. Working on learning solos as they are written will help fuel your own ideas for improvisation.

Lesson 38: The harmonic minor scale

This is another scale that is a great option for shred guitar. A captivating, exotic-sounding scale that is found in various music styles like Jazz, Classical, and Heavy Metal. Making it popular among lead guitarists.

This makes it a favorite among lead guitarists looking to produce this type of emotion. Here, we will learn about the harmonic minor scale, how to create it, and how to fully utilize its potential.

Structure of the Harmonic Minor Scale

The harmonic minor scale is a variation of the natural minor scale. The only difference is that you raise, or sharpen, the 7th tone degree. This alteration introduces a leading tone that adds tension and resolution.

Notice The Difference

A minor scale: A B C D E F G
A harmonic minor scale: A B C D E F G#
A harmonic minor scale formula: 1 2 b3 4 5 b6 7

The natural minor scale has the flat 3rd, 6th, and 7th notes, whereas the harmonic only has the flat 3rd and 6th.

122

Here are a couple of scale pattern examples to work with.

Scale Pattern Example 1:

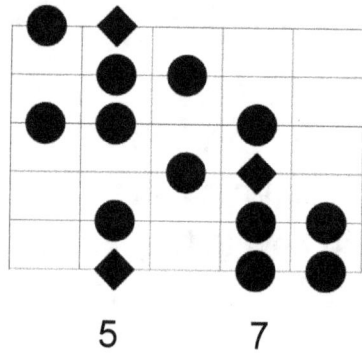

5   7

Here it is at the 5th fret on the 6th string. Go through it and listen to how it sounds.

Scale Pattern Example 2:

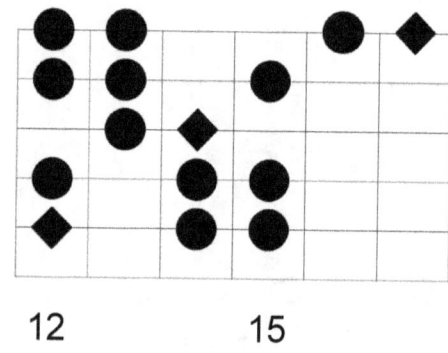

12   15

Here it is at the 12th fret on the 5th string. Play it here as well to get familiar with how it sounds.

What is great about the harmonic minor scale is its distinctive, unique sound quality. This is created through the interval between the 6th and 7th tone degrees.

Notice the whole-step, half-step scale formula, and how the raised or sharpened 7th note makes a difference.

- **Natural minor scale: W - H - W - W - H - W - W**

  1   2   3   4   5   6   7   octave

- **Harmonic minor scale: W - H - W - W - H - W+ H - H**

  1   2   3   4   5   6   7   octave

Notice how the natural minor scale has a whole step between the 6th and 7th tone degree, and the harmonic minor has a whole + half step between them?

It is this specialized note interval that makes the harmonic minor scale so unique, and a worthy addition to your guitar shred toolbox.

Remember, the more scale options you have to play solos, the more you will be able to not only increase your musicianship, but you will also be able to convey mastery over the guitar fretboard.

Harmonic Minor Scale Practice Tips

1. **Practice Slowly:** Begin by playing the scale slowly and accurately. Ensuring that each note rings clearly and efficiently.

2. **Use a metronome:** This will help to develop timing, as well as allow you to gradually increase your speed over time.

3. **Incorporate personality traits:** These are such things as string bends, hammer-ons, pull-offs, slides, vibrato, and trills.

4. **Develop phrasing:** This is where you put your personality traits together to create small pieces of music. When linked together, they create something coherent.

5. **Work on improvising:** As you get familiar with the other 4 tips, you can then work on your original compositions through improvisation.

Learn the scale pattern like you've done with the pentatonics and modes. Create phrasing within it and practice daily. This will allow you to get the most from the harmonic minor scale.

Lesson 39: Sweep picking and arpeggios

Sweep picking is a guitar technique that allows you to play arpeggios smoothly and rapidly by using a continuous sweeping motion with your pick. This technique is widely used in genres like Classical, Jazz, and Heavy Metal.

In this lesson, we'll cover the basics of sweep picking arpeggios and provide some examples and tips to get you started and headed in the right direction.

Using Single Fluid Motion

Sweep picking involves using a single fluid motion to play multiple strings in succession, rather than picking each note individually. When combined with arpeggios, which are notes of a chord played individually, it creates an impressive sound.

Basic Technique:

- **Gripping the pick:** Hold your pick as you normally would, ensuring that it is stable but relaxed. Too firm a grip can impede the motion needed for sweep picking.
- **Hand motion:** Your hand motion should be similar to strumming, but more controlled and precise. Move your hand in a single, smooth motion across the strings.

- **Palm muting:** Use your palm to mute strings after they are played to prevent unwanted string vibration. This is crucial for clarity.
- **Economy of motion:** Minimize hand motion by keeping your fingers close to the fretboard and utilizing minimal hand motion.

Practice Exercises

Exercise #1: Three-string A Major Arpeggio

```
T|-----------------------12---17--------12------------|
A|-----------14---------------------------14----------|
 |------14------------------------------------14------|
B|----------------------------------------------------|
```

In this first example, you use the notes of the A major chord. Starting at the 14th fret on the 3rd string, ascending to the 17th on the 1st, and descending back down again.

Exercise #2: Five-String C Minor Arpeggio

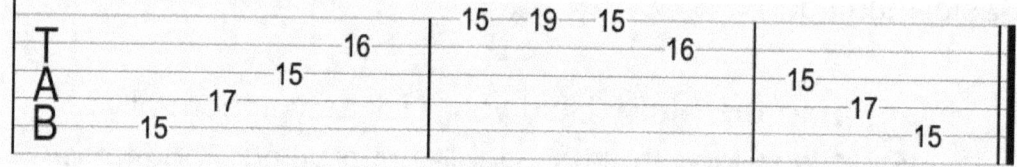

In this second example, you use the notes of the C minor scale. Starting at the 15th fret on the 5th string, ascending to the 19th on the 1st string, and descending back down again.

Exercise #3: Six-String G Major Arpeggio

In this third example, you use the notes of the G major chord. starting at the 10th fret on the 6th string, ascending to the 14th on the 1st string, and descending back down again.

Sweep Picking Tips:

- Start slowly, ensuring that each note rings clearly.

- Gradually increase your speed as you become more comfortable.

- Focus on the continuous motion of your picking hand.

- Use your picking hand to mute strings after they've been played.

- Ensure that each note is individually spaced when playing it.

- Pay close attention to the synchronization between both hands.

Additional Tips For Mastery

- **Develop patience:** Mastering sweep picking requires patience and persistence. Begin with the 1st exercise to get the feel of the technique, then proceed from there.

- **Use a metronome:** This is mandatory; it will help you to develop timing, increase speed, and build self-confidence.

- **Utilize a clean technique:** In the beginning, you need to prioritize clarity over speed. If not, your note will sound muddy, and your technique will show a lack of discipline.

- **Practice consistently:** Only through consistent practice will you be able to develop this skill set. You must incorporate sweep picking into your daily routine.

- **Listen and learn:** You must listen to players who utilize this technique in their playing to fully understand its application. Do this daily.

Sweep picking will require hours of discipline to get right. It can add a dynamic and expressive element to your playing. One that will make people say, **"Wow! How did you do that?"** And that, my friend, is what it's all about.

Lesson 40: Finger tapping & lagato

Finger tapping is a popular guitar technique that adds flair and complexity to your playing. It involves using your picking hand to tap notes on the fretboard, allowing you to play rapid sequences and achieve a unique sound.

Understanding Finger Tapping

Finger tapping is a technique that allows you to reach notes beyond the span of your fretting hand. By tapping with the fingers of the picking hand, you can create fast, fluid runs and arpeggios. Very popular in rock, metal, and classical music.

Basic Technique:

- **Positioning:** Hold your guitar normally, and allow your picking hand to move up and down the fretboard.

- **Tapping motion:** With your index or middle finger, tap on a string with enough force to sound out the note.

- **Pull-off:** After tapping, pull the finger off the string to sound the note your fretting hand is holding.

Use this three-step reference guide to develop this technique.

Practice Exercises:

Exercise #1: Tapping

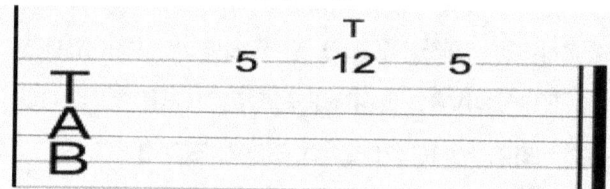

In this example, you play the 5th fret on the 1st string, tap the 12th fret with your picking hand, and pull-off back to the 5th.

Exercise #2: Tapping & pull-off

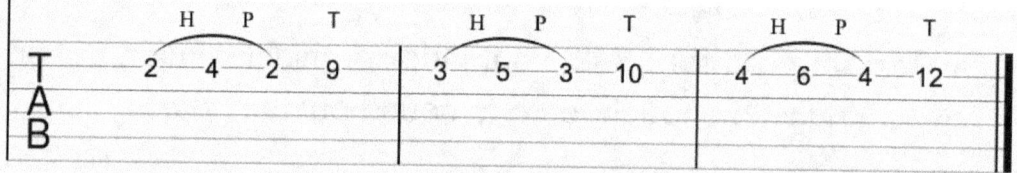

In this example, you move your tapping hand while your fretting hand stays on the same note.

Exercise #3: Hammer-on, pull-off & tapping

In this example, you move both hands as you hammer-on, pull-off, and tap the notes.

Use these examples to get familiar with this technique.

Introduction to Lagato

Lagato is a technique in shred guitar that enables smooth and fluid transitions between notes, resulting in a seamless sound. This technique is essential for achieving speed and precision in your playing.

What is Lagato?

The term "lagato" stands for tied together, and in music terms, it refers to notes being played smoothly together without any interruptions between them. Achieved through hammer-ons, slides, and pull-offs, without picking each note.

Tips for mastering lagato

- Use minimal finger movement to maintain speed and precision.
- Use a metronome to ensure your passages are rhythmically sound.
- Develop finger strength through repeating techniques and exercises.
- Practice, practice, practice.

Remember, patience and consistency are key. By incorporating these techniques into your practice, you'll be well on your way to mastering legato for lead guitar shredding.

Chapter VIII Summary

First, we look at learning from recordings. This not only enhances your listening ability, but it also improves your understanding of how songs are constructed. Learning to play guitar in this method ceases the need for sheet music.

Second, we look at improvising within a song. When improvising, you'll want to identify the key of the song, identify the chords, and identify the scale that you feel will work best for soloing.

Third, we learn about the harmonic minor scale. Another scale that is very popular for shred guitar. The reason is because of the natural 7th note that makes it sound exotic and gives it a very distinct tone.

Fourth, we learn sweep picking and arpeggios. Sweep picking is where you sweep the pick across the strings playing multiple notes, and an arpeggio is where you play the notes of a chord individually.

Lastly, we learn about finger tapping and legato. Two other very popular techniques in shred guitar. Finger tapping is using your picking hand to tap notes on the fretboard, and legato is using hammer-ons, pull-offs, and slides to create fluidity.

Lead Guitar Shredder: Conclusion

If you've made it this far, I congratulate you on your accomplishments and say, "Thank you for your purchase of this book and your time learning to play what I have taught". You seem like the kind of student that I'd love to teach in person.

Chapter 1 is all about the basics of lead guitar. Types of lead guitars, types of amplifiers, reading guitar tabs, and learning finger exercises. All these things will provide you with a solid foundation on which to build.

Chapter 2 is about learning the five minor pentatonic scale patterns. These will allow you to build a road map along the fretboard. This will help you to stay in key, as well as develop mastery over the guitar fretboard.

Chapter 3 is about learning the five major pentatonic scale patterns. These will allow you to do the same as the minor, but also allow you to know where to play over major chord progressions.

Chapter 4 is about adding the blue note. The flat 5th. This allows you to add tension and dissonance, creating a bluesy tone with emotional depth. These chromatic notes can add a sense of darkness and sadness.

Chapter 5 is about establishing personality traits. These are your hammer-ons, pull-offs, slides, bends, trills, and vibrato. Also, triplets, melodic shapes, alternate, and tremolo picking. All needed for proficient lead guitar shredding.

Chapter 6 is about phrasing with guitar licks. Learn what they are and how to create them within the five minor scale patterns. These can be applied to any scales you choose to learn, and these are what solos are made up of.

Chapter 7 is about the seven modes of the major scale. The Ionian, Dorian, Lydian, Mixolydian, Aeolian, and Locrian. These are very popular for soloing and can give you a variety of options due to their note intervals.

Chapter 8 is about additional training. Such things as learning from recordings, improvising, the harmonic minor scale, sweep picking arpeggios, legato, and finger tapping. If you need help with any of this, feel free to contact me at my website below.

www.DwaynesGuitarLessons.com

To all your success,
Sincerely, Dwayne Jenkins

Other Books From Tritone Publishing

Guitar Modes: Unlock The Secrets

Dive deeper into the modes of the major scale with this easy to learn from, comprehensive guidebook. Modes can add a rich vocabulary for both harmony and melody.

Guitar Modes: Unlock The Secrets will allow you to expand your improvisation skills, enhance your chord vocabulary, and deepen your understanding of music theory.

Learn To Play Rhythm Guitar:

A comprehensive training course for learning chords, chord progressions, strumming, arpeggiated picking, and all things needed to be a great rhythm guitar player.

With a step-by-step system and your desire to learn, you'll be playing quickly and easily. Before you know it, you will increase your musicianship and understanding of timing and rhythm.

Learn Guitar Chord Theory:

Have you ever looked at notation and wondered what a Cadd9 chord is? Or possibly a Gsus4? If you have, this book will explain what it is, how to create it, and how to use it.

Learn Guitar Chord Theory is a comprehensive study guide on the inner workings of guitar chords. Take the time to develop your chord vocabulary and mix it with a full understanding of how they work, and you'll become a much better player.

138

All books are authored by Dwayne Jenkins, published by Tritone Publishing, and can be found worldwide.

Digital formats of all titles are also available for quicker learning. Just download them onto your computer and start learning right away.

Self-study is a great way to learn, as it allows you to not only go at your own pace but also develop the skills of self-discipline and time management. Which can benefit you in other areas of your life.

Also, check out Dwayne's Guitar Lessons video channel on YouTube. These are free lessons that cover a wide variety of topics related to playing the guitar.

Whether you are working on rhythm, lead, theory, or guitar maintenance, it is all here in these lessons. These are available 24 hours a day, 7 days a week, 365 days a year.

And if more help is needed, Dwayne also offers one-on-one private coaching. Which can be found on his website.

DwaynesGuitarLessons.com

Best of luck, and have fun.

About the Author

Dwayne Jenkins is a professional guitar teacher, an accomplished musician, and an entrepreneur. He has been learning, playing, and teaching guitar lessons throughout Denver, CO, for over two decades.

He is now bringing his special training skills and methodology that have been honed and hand-crafted throughout the years on how to play to students around the world.

Dwayne has a unique, exciting approach that gets students of all ages and skill levels enjoying the fun of playing guitar and ukulele. His enthusiasm and love for teaching shine through every lesson that he creates.

His lessons are designed to enhance your ability to progress. No matter your reason for learning, there will always be something in Dwayne's books and products to help you achieve your dreams.

So if you're a student looking to start or a student looking to further your education, be sure to get involved with Dwayne's guitar lessons and learn what so many people have already discovered: why learning to play the guitar or ukulele is one of the greatest things you can do for yourself.

What Students Are Saying About Dwayne's Guitar Lessons

"Dwayne, thank you so much for everything you have taught me and done for me. You are an amazing guitarist and wonderful teacher". BJ

"Dwayne, it has been a true pleasure to have you at our house each week! Ken & Trevor have learned so much through you and your teachings. Thank you!" Lisa

"Dwayne, thank you for being a great teacher and teaching me many great songs. This is a skill that will last me a lifetime." Danielle

"Dwayne, we want you to know we are honored to have you at the studio. We appreciate all that you do and are grateful that we can leave you in charge." Angie & Wilson M.E.C.

"Dwayne, we are so glad you are our Teacher. It's been three years already, can you believe it? Thank you again. You're the best!" Chelsey & Lucas.

"Dwayne, we are so glad that you are in our lives. Chelsey & Lucas enjoy their time with you and look up to you. Looking forward to another great year!" Love and best wishes, Ken & Sue.

142

"Dwayne, thank you so much for being not only an awesome guitar teacher but an awesome friend as well," Kayla said.

"Dwayne, thank you so much for all the years of doing lessons. You have been very patient with my progress, helped me to build confidence in myself, and inspired me to follow my dreams. And in doing so, you have become a great friend." Jake.

.

"Dwayne, thank you for teaching Nick guitar so well. He loves it and is getting quite good fast. I'm amazed!" Jane.

"Dwayne, thank you so much for teaching me every Saturday, and not only teaching me guitar but also about life and helping me with setting my goals. You are a great teacher, mentor, and the best friend ever." Carson.

"There is no other person I would want to teach me a guitar! His 1-on-1 teaching makes learning guitar very personal & exhilarating. He teaches at your pace and takes pride in what YOU want to learn. The best part is that if Dwayne doesn't know a song a student wants to play, he takes time out of the week to learn it. His teaching comes to life in my performance and has progressed over the last 8 years. Words cannot describe how amazing a teacher, rockstar, and true friend Dwayne has become to me." Dominic.